The
Tiferet
Talk Interviews

MELISSA STUDDARD

Introduction by Donna Baier Stein

Published by
Tiferet Press
211 Dryden Rd.
Bernardsville, NJ 07924
www.tiferetjournal.com

Cover design: Allen Mohr
Book editing and design: Diane Bonavist
Interview transcription: Valerie Alba
BlogTalkRadio coordination: Michelle Mangen
Author photos, where credits are not indicated, were supplied by the author or
are obtainable online.

ISBN: 0615737595
ISBN 13: 9780615737591
Library of Congress Control Number: 2012955566

CONTENTS

INTRODUCTION

Imagine joining intimate conversations with a brilliant and eclectic bunch of writers, thinkers, and people eager to improve the world. That's what this volume invites you to do. Here are twelve interviews conducted by host Melissa Studdard on our Tiferet Talk radio programs.

Robert Pinsky, former poet laureate of the United States; Julia Cameron, author of *The Artist's Way*; Edward Hirsch, chancellor of the American Academy of Poets and president of the Guggenheim Foundation; Robin Rice, spiritual teacher and internationally-published author; Dr. Bernie Siegel, inspiring author and global speaker; and more.

The interviewees share their thoughts on ways to tell the truth of our lives, access creativity, and balance magic and craft.

Before you begin reading, let me tell you how *Tiferet: Literature, Art, & The Creative Spirit* came to exist. It began with my learning a new word: *tiferet*. This is a Hebrew word that, in my opinion, describes a state from which true creativity arises. I think of it as being similar to the razor's edge envisioned by Somerset Maugham—a balancing of heaven and earth, good and evil, opposing forces that don't usually reconcile. On the Tree of Life, *tiferet* is a stable center where the physical and spiritual realms meet.

Just as a word led to my decision to create a multi-faith literary magazine, it can be no accident that the Word holds such significance in many world religions and spiritual practices. "In the beginning was the Word," proclaims John 1:1 in the New Testament. According to Jewish mysticism, there is divine mystery behind the drawing and placement of each letter in the alphabet. In Hinduism, the letters of the alphabet are forms of the goddesses Matrikas.

And as former Nobel Peace Prize winner Shirin Ebadi noted, "The first sermon in Islam begins with the word 'Recite'.... The Koran swears by the pen and what it writes. Such a sermon and message cannot be in conflict with awareness, knowledge, wisdom, freedom of opinion and expression and cultural pluralism."

Her list of desired qualities includes my own hope for *Tiferet: Literature, Art, & The Creative Spirit* and Tiferet Talk: an increase in awareness, creative expression, and cultural pluralism.

May these transcribed and edited interviews, conducted with such warmth and insight by host Melissa Studdard, spark your own flames of creativity. You are also invited to join our global community of writers fostering creativity and peace in the individual and the world by visiting us at www.tiferetjournal.com.

Donna Baier Stein, Publisher
Tiferet: Literature, Art, & The Creative Spirit

THE TIFERET TALK
INTERVIEWS

Photograph by Aloma

JULIA CAMERON

JUNE 15, 2010

MELISSA: Julia Cameron is an award-winning poet, playwright, filmmaker and novelist who has published over thirty books. In addition to her own prolific output, she is also a celebrated mentor, teacher, and guide to many others, through her workshops and best-selling books on creativity. *The Artist's Way* has sold over four million copies world-wide, and her follow-up best sellers, *The Vein of Gold*, *Walking in this World*, and *The Right to Write* are also considered seminal texts on the creative process. Advocating creativity as an authentic spiritual path, Cameron's work has been embraced by diverse spiritual and religious groups around the globe and is widely taught in both academic and grass-roots settings. Thank you so much for joining us. We are looking forward to a fantastic exploration of the creative process. Julia, how are you doing this afternoon?

JULIA: Good. I spent my morning down at the Chelsea Studios watching a run through of my roommate's new musical. So, I've had a very creative day so far.

MELISSA: I'd like to start by asking you a pretty basic question about creativity, so your morning is a good lead-in to that. As you know, there are many people who are skeptical about whether or not creativity can be taught, and I think you would say that what you do is actually teach people to access their creativity. Will you explain how this works and what some of the basic tools are—like Morning Pages and the Artist's Date?

JULIA: Well, first of all, I want to say that I don't run into too much skepticism. But, you know, I occasionally will get someone who says to me, "Julia, aren't you afraid you're unlocking an awful lot of bad art?" And what I have to say to them is that actually my experience is just the opposite. When people are unblocked, it turns out that there are many absolutely wonderful artists who do beautiful work. Then you find yourself wondering how they could ever have been blocked. They were so wonderful.

So, I went to the reading this morning, and one of the actresses at the reading, who was just brilliant, came up to me at the break and said, "I'm halfway through your book, and I'm dying to talk to you." So, I don't think I teach creativity for dummies. I think that I do teach that we are all creative, and that has been my experience for twenty-five years. I have never run across someone who was genuinely noncreative. But some of us have an easier time of tapping into it.

MELISSA: Would you do a quick explanation of the Morning Pages and the Artist's Date for people who aren't familiar with it already?

JULIA: I'd like to actually explain three tools. The first tool is Morning Pages, and this is the bedrock tool of a creative recovery. It's three pages of long-hand

I have never run across someone who was genuinely non-creative.

morning writing that you do first thing when you wake up, and it can be about anything. So, it's sort of like, "Good morning. Today I'm grumpy," or "Good morning, I forgot to call my sister back," and "I didn't buy kitty litter." It can be about anything. You just let your pen sort of skitter across the page for three pages. Morning Pages are a form, I would say, really, of prayer and meditation. We are notifying the universe what we like and what we don't like, what we want more of and what we want less of. We are sending out a little telegram "dot, dotta, dot, dot, dot, dot." And Morning Pages are private. They shouldn't be shown to anybody. They are simply you and your thoughts. What they do is they miniaturize the internal censor or the critic—because when you do your Morning Pages, your critic will start babbling at you and start saying, "Oh, you are so negative," "Oh, you are so grumpy," and you just say to the critic, "Thank you for sharing," and you keep right on writing. This trains your censor that it has to learn to step aside and let you create.

So, that's Morning Pages. What we're really trying to do is build a radio kit. So, the first tool, Morning Pages, is sending. The second tool is a tool called Artist's Date, and it's a tool of receiving. Once a week, you go out by yourself and do something that's festive and interesting to you. It doesn't have to be high art; it just has to be something that catches your fancy.

I have a lot of people who say that they got a manicure and that was their Artist's Date. It was something that made them feel spoiled. What happens with an Artist's Date is that you start to get intuitions, and you begin to get answers for the questions that you have posed in your Morning Pages.

The third tool, which I didn't know when I wrote The Artist's Way, was buried in a week twelve exercise. After I taught for another decade, I realized it should be right up there with the basic tools, so when I teach now, which I do every Wednesday, I have a handout that says you will take two twenty minute walks.

When people walk, they integrate. So, they might walk out with a problem, but they might walk back with a solution. It's hard to stay feeling overwhelmed when you're walking.

A lot of my tools are tools that people instinctively use. All I've done is made them very clear and deliberate.

MELISSA: The way you've done it has reached out to a lot of people, though. Even if they've been doing it instinctively on some level, now they have a format to follow for when they do get blocked. They can go back and look at this and know what to do.

In fact, you talked earlier about artists who've become unblocked through this—do you have any favorite success stories about people who have gone on to create things that they later told you about?

JULIA: I was in Colorado Springs, and I was invited to go see a juried show. There were like two thousand pieces. You know how it is when you see those juried shows? A lot of times you don't like the art they picked. What happened was that I absolutely loved the first place winner, and I wanted to meet her.

I was shown over to a girl, and she said, "Yes, I did this work," and I said, "Oh, it's so wonderful." She said, "Well, what do you do?" I told her I was a writer, and she asked if I'd written anything she would know. I told her I'd written a book called *The Artist's Way*, and she said, "Oh, my God! I was blocked for twenty years, and I picked up your book, and here I am now, winning the juried show." She said, "But you really want to talk to the girl who came in second." And so I looked around and saw the second-place art, and I also really loved it, and she said, "She's not here right now, but if she were, she would tell you she was my college roommate. I mailed her the book." I have quite a few stories like that.

MELISSA: One of the things that interests me about that particular story is they're not writers, they're visual artists. I think some people assume that because writing is one of the main tools that the process might be just for writers, but you have actually said that sometimes it's the writers who have the most difficulty with the Morning Pages because they try to write them stylistically and make them artistic when that's not what they are really about. Is that right?

JULIA: Right. Morning Pages are really just a housekeeping tool. It's like you take a little whisk broom to your consciousness, and you stick it in all the corners of things that are troubling you, and you whisk them out into the center of the floor where you can look at them.

When people write in journals they typically set a topic and say, "I'm going to write everything I feel about my mother." And then they write on their mother for three pages. When you do Morning Pages, you don't set any topics. So, it's as though you have ADD. You go topic to topic, to topic, to topic—skittering all over the map.

MELISSA: Is it important to do the Morning Pages in the morning? I mean, obviously they are called Morning Pages, but …

JULIA: Right. I sometimes think I should say I've been teaching for twenty-five years, and I was wrong, and I should now call them Evening Pages. But, the truth is that Morning Pages are "Morning Pages" because

> *It's like you take a little whisk broom to your consciousness, and you stick it in all the corners of things that are troubling you, and you whisk them out into the center of the floor where you can look at them.*

they prioritize the day you are going to have, and if you do them later in the day, you're talking about a day you already had and that you are powerless to change.

MELISSA: You were talking earlier about how you teach every Wednesday, and I know a lot of our listeners are teachers and professors and writers and artists too. At times, I think, it can feel like they are giving away so much of their own creative energy to teaching that they don't feel like they have much left for their own art.

You've been a wonderful model for how to create that balance between mentoring and creating so that the activities not only coexist but actually enhance each other. What kind of advice would you give others who are looking for that harmony between teaching and making art?

JULIA: It's going to sound self-serving, but I would say work *The Artist's Way*—because if you're doing an Artist's Date every week, it's hard to be too martyred. If you are consciously dealing with your own creativity on a daily basis, you start to draw different boundaries with other people, and if you're out walking, you are going to come to your own thoughts eventually. You might walk out feeling sort of grumpy, but then you walk a little ways, and you notice the wonderful petunias in the window box or the great calico cat, or you go over to the park and see the squirrels sitting on Ramrod Street waving their tails at you.

So, if you use The Artist's Way tool kit, it goes a long way toward dismantling what I call the "virtue trap." The virtue trap is when people are too self-sacrificing. A lot of teachers have to learn how to nurture themselves. I've often said that they need to stick to the basic tools, and when they do, they will be rewarded.

MELISSA: I think the last thing you could be accused of is being self-serving. For one thing, at the end of The Artist's Way, you recommend that once people have read the book they should just pass it on, and you make it clear you're not interested in making money—that you're just interested in helping people to make their art.

JULIA: Thank you. When *The Artist's Way* came out, I had an opportunity to franchise it—the people who had franchised "est" approached me and wanted to franchise *The Artist's Way*, and I said no and that I thought it should be free. I do think people should be able to just start a group with a book.

MELISSA: The whole process, the way you presented it, is very democratic, and the idea is that anyone can have a group, and there really shouldn't necessarily be a group leader. You don't have to be trained to run a group.

Anyone can make art, maybe not great art, maybe not the specific art they want to make, but everyone can make something. I think that's one of the things that made the book successful—that and the fact that obviously you are a practitioner. You talk about that a lot in *Floor Sample*. Can you read the beginning of that to us?

JULIA: The late afternoon sky is pewter. Wind whips through the Manhattan canyons. In Central Park, a single large gingko tree stands golden against the glowering clouds. Underfoot are the thickly fallen leaves of maple, oak and ash. Gusts of wind send the leaves dancing. Dog owners like myself hurry their charges on their rounds. It is nearly Thanksgiving, and the dark comes early.

Perhaps because of all my school years, fall for me is a time of beginnings. The short, steep days send me tumbling into my past. I am fifty-seven years of age, neither old nor young. My life has swept me along on its tide, but now, at the midpoint, it is time to pick my way along the shoreline, to see what of value has been washed up, which mementos should be pocketed and which cast aside. Mine has been a turbulent life. But it did not start out that way.

I grew up in Libertyville, Illinois, in a large yellow house in the woods. An oversized, overstuffed English cottage, the house was made of fieldstone and wood. Cold pried at the windows. Dark gathered in the surrounding trees. As early as late September, fires were built in the three fireplaces to ward off the chill. Just outside the front door stood a large maple tree. When its leaves turned crimson, my mother would carefully press the best between sheets of waxed paper. These leaves were then tacked on our kitchen bulletin board amid vivid charcoal drawings of Halloween.

Fall was fierce, but my mother domesticated it. As the wind stripped the trees, my mother made simmering pots of vegetable soup. She baked shortbreads and berry pies. As early as October, she began her holiday baking, filling the downstairs freezer with a dozen different Christmas cookies, divinity, and fudge.

"Let's go to your house," my school friends would say. Of course they did. Homemade cookies and frosty mile were staple after-school fare. If we felt daring, we raided the freezer. Christmas cookies tasted best a month or two before their time. "Who's been after the Christmas cookies?" my mother would interrogate us, but she always seemed secretly pleased by the chance to bake some more.

When winter displaced fall, reading spots in front of the fire-places were at a premium. The best locale was in our living room. There the reader could loll on thick café-au-lait carpet-ing. A mesh screen protected errant bookworms from flying sparks. Prodded by a wrought-iron poker, the fire could be built to a snapping roar, so hot that clothing singed. "Don't crawl in the fire," my mother would warn. Pajamas were the favored gear. What could be more idyllic than flannel pajamas and a new volume of Nancy Drew? Even better, the latest volume by Marguerite Henry, *Misty of Chincoteague*, Sea Star, *Brightly of the Grand Canyon*, or *King of the Wind*. Ours was a house filled with books.

Just off the kitchen, the den was a snug reading room with floor-to-ceiling bookcases. Here were found the classics: *Crime and Punishment*, *A Tale of Two Cities*, *Oliver Twist*, *Gulliver's Travels*, and rows more. The books in this room were leather-bound and gleamed in the light of the brass lamp that hung suspended from the ceiling. An overstuffed sofa, ideal for sprawling, ran wall to wall, bookcase to window. The only other furniture was Mother's writing desk and a straight-backed chair.

It was in the den that I first discovered Lawrence of Arabia, striding through the pages of his memoirs. His hot Arabia was accompanied by cool jazz. Hidden behind a magic wooden panel, the stereo played Dave Brubeck for my father or, if my mother did the programming, "The Nutcracker Suite." I went through an obsessive phase when all I wanted to hear was Ravel's "Bolero." I choreographed my sisters and brothers dancing and dying. "Either change the music or change the ending," my mother pressed me. I went back to reading.

Upstairs, in the long hallway that ran between the bedrooms, there was another floor-to ceiling bookcase—and this one was not for classics. Here was the family cache of mysteries and big, popular potboilers like *Exodus, The Listener, and Dear and Glorious Physician*. Here was my brothers' stash of Hardy Boys and my older sister Connie's Nancy Drews. I do not know that I read every book, but I do know that I tried. I still remember the guilty exhilaration I felt racing through the *Reader's Digest Condensed Books*, three tales to a volume.

Augmenting the books we owned were the books we borrowed. Once weekly my mother would load us in the car, a navy blue Vista

Cruiser station wagon, and drive us the two miles to Cook Memorial Library, where we were allowed to take out fourteen books apiece, two per day. The library was a mansion donated to the village. It rose snow white and stately amid splendid rose gardens. Outside and in, it was a place of enchantment. The horse books were upstairs on the second floor, front. There, Walter Farley reigned supreme: *The Black Stallion, The Island Stallion, The Island Stallion Races*...I read them all.

I had a limitless appetite for horse books, and for books of all stripes, for that matter.

MELISSA: It's so wonderful for people who are using your advice on how to write to actually hear your writing. So, do you mind explaining the concept of yourself as the floor sample?

JULIA: The way *The Artist's Way* came about was that I, in 1978, got sober. I'd spent ten years drinking and writing, and I had a lot of confusion in those days with alcoholism and artistry because many of our role models were alcoholics. So, you think, well drinking and writing go together like scotch and soda, but I finally recognized that the drinking was getting in the way of the writing and that I had to find a way to write sober.

I began trying to let something write through me, and I discovered that if I tried to let a creative force work through me that I was able to write much more freely. As soon as I figured this out, I told it to my sister, who was a painter, and she tried to let something paint through her, and we quickly discovered that the tools that worked to keep me unblocked as a person would work for other people as well.

I come from a large family of seven kids, and whenever you would learn something, you would teach it to your siblings. And so, I think, that's what happened with The Artist's Way. I learned something, and I turned around to teach to my siblings, who are fellow artists.

MELISSA: What compelled you to write *Floor Sample*? What lead you to realize that you wanted to, or felt like it was a good time to tell your own story?

JULIA: What I'm trying to teach people is that they can make contact with the benevolent creative force, and that's a personal thing, and everybody can have free access to it. One of the things I wanted to do was step out from behind.

Sometimes people have a tendency to want a magic teacher, some-body who is all-wise and all-knowing and has no problems, just like a fairy godmother. I wanted to say, "No, I'm really an artist among artists, and my tools work for me because they have had to work for me because I've had a turbulent life."

When *Floor Sample* came out, the first review said I was an unfit mother.

MELISSA: That's the bad criticism that we don't listen to, right?

JULIA: Well, it was just ruthless. And I wondered what book they read since my daughter and I are very close and always lived together and worked together. She came to the reading with me this morning. So, anyway, I wanted to step down off the pedestal, and I thought that was healthy. And I do think that it is a healthy book for people.

MELISSA: Yes, I think so too. It is just so beautifully written, and it's honest and direct. Will you also read a couple of passages from *Faith and Will: Weathering the Storms in Our Spiritual Lives*, your new book that was excerpted in the June 2010 edition of Tiferet?

Our job is to cooperate. That is to co-operate. To work with the intentions of the higher force that wishes something to be expressed. We may conceptualize this higher force as either art or writing, music or painting, it doesn't really matter what we name it. What matters is that when it touches our consciousness we yield the right of way.

JULIA: Both Brahms and Puccini credited God with being the source of their flow of musical ideas. For both men, the term creator was quite literal. God was the great creator; they were the channel through which he worked. It was for them that simple and that workable. It can be that simple and workable for us if we will allow it. When artists speak of being the servant of their art, this is what we mean. Something larger or grander than ourselves seems to be working through us. Our job is to cooperate. That is to co-operate. To work with the intentions of the higher force that wishes something to be expressed. We may conceptualize this higher force as either art or writing, music or painting, it doesn't really matter what we name it. What matters is that when it touches our consciousness we yield the right of way. There is a sort of inner door that we alone can swing open. This door once nudged open can allow us to perceive what we may call higher realms.

MELISSA: Can you elaborate on that a bit? I think this concept may be new to some people—the idea of a conduit or co-creator replacing the antiquated image you mentioned earlier of the lone artist with the ancient typewriter and a bottle of scotch.

JULIA : I know the cliché because I lived the cliché.

MELISSA: But you overcame it. How are we co-creators with God in making art, and how can we tap into and access that in a practical way? I mean, how do we just step aside and let that happen? I think a lot of people get in the way of their own art.

JULIA: Again, I'm going to send people back to the basic tools. If you write your Morning Pages, and your censor objects, as your censor will, and you say to your censor, "there's no wrong way to do this," and you keep on writing, that becomes a portable skill. Then when you sit down to write something else, and your censor rears its head and says this isn't any good, you can say to your censor, "Thank you for sharing, but I'm going to keep right on writing," or "I'm going to keep right on painting."

MELISSA: Can you talk about synchronicity as a byproduct of co-creation and how that works?

JULIA: Well, one of the things that happens when we start working with the radio kit is that we begin to find ourselves in the right time and in the right place, and we begin to experience, if you will, what I would call a "higher octave." I'll give an example.

I went on an Artist's Date to a book store called The Complete Traveler, and in the back of the store, I saw a shelf full of books that were like fifty years old. I saw one on Magellan, and I took it down, and just on a whim I bought the book. Then I left on a book tour and took the book with me, and I opened it up when I was in Los Angeles in a hotel called the Shangri-La, which overlooked the Pacific Ocean. I read a little bit of Magellan and looked out at the ocean, and then I fell asleep, and when I woke up I suddenly had a head full of music. That started me writing music that occupied me for a decade.

MELISSA: You've been so prolific, and you've written in so many different genres. Is there a specific genre that is easiest for you? Does the work let you know what format it's going to be in? How does that work for you?

JULIA: Usually they tell you what they are pretty fast.

MELISSA: At the beginning?

JULIA: Yes, it will say, "I'm a play." And you find yourself writing a play. I can't emphasize enough that if you use the tools, you will find yourself getting unblocked in many different stripes. I was on book tour when I got the idea for my novel *Mozart's Ghost*, which is newly out in paperback.

MELISSA: I love that book. When I first looked at the cover and saw Erica Jong's comment that it was "heartbreakingly funny," I just thought, "Well, how on earth could something be 'heartbreakingly funny?'"

Then I started reading and discovered this woman, this character, who believes she'd been dumped by the man who's upstairs practicing his piano 24/7. So she has to sit there all day listening to this beautiful music coming from this man who broke her heart, and it is literally "heartbreakingly funny."

It's full of metaphors and examples of your own theories for making art. The medium is sort of a metaphor for channeling creativity. Mrs. Murphy is an artistic mentor, the letters in short chapters are like the bursts of Morning Pages, and the pianist works through intense artistic resistance. Were these things operating at a conscious level for you when you were writing the book, or did they just naturally unfold?

JULIA: I was on book tour when I started writing the book, and I couldn't do any research for it while going city to city, hotel room to hotel room, so I made up rules for myself that everything in the book had to come from what was already in my consciousness.

MELISSA: Well, it worked out beautifully. The characters are so compelling. I mean, when I finished, I wondered if there would be a sequel because I wanted to learn more about the characters. Have you thought about that yet?

JULIA: Well, I wrote a sequel, and hopefully, someday, somebody's going to want to publish it. But first of all, people have to read *Mozart's Ghost* in sufficient numbers to justify a sequel.

MELISSA: Well, I definitely recommend it to anyone who's listening. I enjoyed it thoroughly.

JULIA: Thank you. I loved writing it. I had a very, very good time.

MELISSA: You're welcome. That's the best way, isn't it? Would you say that that's one of the things that alerts you that you really are in active co-creating—that you are enjoying it at that level?

JULIA: Well, I think you get sort of tickled, you know, to use an old-fashioned word for it. You're writing and you go, "Oh!" You have a little bit of a sense of surprise as the work unfolds.

MELISSA: Right. Yes, definitely. I am going to let a caller through.

CALLER: This is Jeffrey Davis.

MELISSA: Thank you for calling. It's good to hear from you.

JEFFREY: It's good to hear you, Melissa. And, Julia, thank you for this interview. I have a brief question that comes from a book you wrote several years ago called *The Right to Write*, which I enjoyed so much. I pick it up often, and one particular chapter that resonated with me was on vulnerability, which is not something many writers really talk about. I just wanted to ask you to elaborate on it.

As more and more of us take to the page, we explore and express our honest vulnerabilities, and we become more open to the human condition in ourselves and others. You talk about how in that process we render ourselves compassionate and discover that what we have begun to say is only the beginning of "righting" things. I'm making a pun there. So, I just wanted to hear more of your thoughts about compassion, which is a subject dear to my heart in writing—how we know we're "writing rightly," so to speak, and how that is related to compassion in your practice?

JULIA: I think the first thing is tenderness. All too often when we set about looking at ourselves we feel that we've come up short, and we judge ourselves very harshly and tell ourselves things like, "I should be doing more of this."

When you start to have more tenderness, you begin to say to yourself, "How do you really feel? What are you really interested by? What are you frightened by? What's keeping you from the page?"

I have an exercise called "blasting through blocks." It's in the back part of *The Artist's Way*. It's an exercise where you write down what your fears and your angers and your resentments are about that piece of work you need to do and make the act of putting these things on the page an act of vulnerability. As you do that, it frees you to write.

JEFFREY: I can see that. It renders you even more open. Thank you.

MELISSA: I have a question about deadlines. Do you have any special advice for people who are working with deadlines on how to stay open and not get cramped up—something that would keep them from getting in that position where they feel like they just have to hammer something out that may even be a little artificial?

JULIA: The tool that specifically relates to this is taking an Artist's Date. What the Artist's Date does is refill the well, and when you make a piece of art, whether its painting, photography, or writing, you are fishing out of an inner well for images.

When you're on a deadline, the temptation is to skip your Artist's Date and "bear down," and instead, what I would say is to double your Artist's Date. Try and take an extra one because you are fishing from the well, and what you want to do is get images back in the well so that when you go to scoop them out they come out more easily.

MELISSA: You have been such an amazing mentor, an inspiration, to so many other people. Is there anyone in particular who was an inspiration or mentor for you?

JULIA: Oh, yes. I've had some wonderful ones. I had a director friend named John Newland, and Newland was a very bold and brave director, and he loved my plays. We worked together sev-

> *Believing mirrors are people who mirror back to you your own potential and your strength, and if you tell them, "I'm going to try something," they say, "I bet you can do it."*

eral times, and then he died. Before he died he said to me "You will always be able to reach me, Julia."

And then I have a wonderful mentor and friend named Juliana McCarthy. Juliana is an actress. And another actress friend named Jane Cecil. I'm sort of selfish—Juliana is on California time, and Jane is on New York time, so I have support 24/7.

I also have a girlfriend named Sonia Choquette, who you might want to interview. She's a wonderful psychic. I helped her with getting her writing career launched. She helps me stay on track. If I call her up and say I feel a little entrapment she will say, "You're doing fine. Ask Spirit to make you larger."

MELISSA: Can you talk about the importance of community for the artist?

JULIA: I couldn't talk about anything that mattered more. That type of question is what *The Artist's Way* aims at. It is creating community.

I have a phrase that I use called "believing mirrors." Believing mirrors are people who mirror back to you your own potential and your strength, and if you tell them, "I'm going to try something," they say, "I bet you can do it."

So, for me: Jane, Juliana, John, Sonia, and my sister, Libby, who was the first painter to get unblocked using the tools.

MELISSA: It's so important for people to not be off in a room by themselves trying to create and not having that support. It can make the difference between something coming to light and not coming to light.

JULIA: Yeah, and they are very important in that they are able to believe in you when you are unable to believe in yourself.

MELISSA: That's an excellent point.

JULIA: *Mozart's Ghost* kept getting almost bought. An editor would fall in love with it but wouldn't be able to get it through committee. This went on endlessly, and I was getting very discouraged. Sonia, the psychic friend of mine, kept saying, "Julia, I see this book. I see it getting published. Keep trying, and keep trying." And we kept trying, and finally, St. Martin's Press and another press both wanted it.

MELISSA: Perfect.

JULIA: But, that was after quite a few turn downs.

MELISSA: That's a wonderful story for people who are just getting started as artists and writers to hear because they probably think, "Oh, if I just had a successful book like *The Artist's Way*, I could write anything and publish it and they would be clamoring." It's good to know it's just case by case and that we are all out there trying to get our work heard and read.

We have another caller.

CALLER: Hi, Melissa. It's Donna.

MELISSA: Donna is our publisher.

DONNA: Julia, thank you so much for being on the show.

JULIA: You are very welcome.

DONNA: Your book, *The Artist's Way*, was a milestone in my life many years ago, and I saw you last year at The Omega Institute. Your teaching in person is as influential and kind and compassionate as your writing is in your books. Can you speak for a moment about comparing speaking to a class to writing and whether you are opening yourself up the way that you do when you write on the computer or on paper?

JULIA: It's an interesting thing. Before I teach, I always pray: "Dear God, let me do a good job; let me be of service. Please tell me what you want me to teach tonight."

And I never get an answer. It's like radio silence. And I get scared and then I get up to teach, and right as I am standing there to teach, I get an intuition. And so it never seems to come early. It seems to come exactly when it's needed, and so it very much becomes a moment by moment process. In that sense it's very similar to writing. I basically think that both teaching and writing are forms of listening. You're keeping your ear tapped to see what wants to come through you. So, I feel that they are very similar.

DONNA: So, you don't do much planning then before you give a lecture?

JULIA: I do. I do planning, but it goes out the window.

DONNA: Well, I know that at the workshop last spring it was wonderful. You broke us into small groups, and I saw people who had not done any writing before just blossom, and they were producing, and I thank you again just for being there and helping me and so many other writers.

JULIA: You are very welcome, and when I break people into clusters, I get them to listen to each other.

DONNA: That was a wonderful experience. I still have friends from my little clusters last spring.

JULIA: See, that's the point. I teach Wednesday nights at the Open Center here in New York, and classes come together, and sometimes they want to hear from me, and I say, "No, really, we want to hear from you." It's a training process of getting them to trust the tools and trust each other and to find that they are definitely led—and that there is synchronicity involved in who they are sitting with.

JULIA: I'm hoping that your enthusiasm for *Mozart's Ghost* may mean that some people will explore that.

MELISSA: I hope so too. Thank you for being with us today. I can't tell you what a pleasure it was to talk to you. You've been such an inspiration to so many people.

JUDE RITTENHOUSE

AUGUST 17, 2010

MELISSA: Our interview tonight is with award-winning poet, Nondual Kabbalistic Healer®, and featured Tiferet blogger, Jude Rittenhouse. Rittenhouse has received various fiction and poetry awards, and her work has been published widely in literary magazines. In addition to writing, freelance editing, and working with individuals in her holistic practice, Rittenhouse teaches and lectures in a variety of settings, such as conferences, retreats, schools, hospitals and alternative health centers. She has a master's degree in counseling and says that, in all of her endeavors, she strives to empower others as they explore their unique journeys towards wholeness. Rittenhouse's second collection of poems, *Living in Skin,* was released as a chapbook in 2009.

Gray Jacobik has said, "As I was reading the poems in Jude Rittenhouse's *Living in Skin*, I found myself repeating, again and again, the first two lines from one of Dickinson's: 'I am afraid to own a Body/I am afraid to own a Soul.' Like Dickinson, Rittenhouse lives on the edge of experience: both extremes, the ecstatic and the horrific, thus her poems are capacious and tenderly human. They are informed by what Genpo Roshi calls "Big Mind." This means: varied subjects and tones, coherent, informing vision, organic structure, authentic speech. It's the juice I read for."

So, my question is this, Jude: Can you start by speaking about this all-encompassing approach in your poems and how you perceive the idea of an informing vision in your work?

JUDE: First I'd like to say how honored I am to have had those words written about my work by Gray Jacobik, who is an extraordinary poet. In fact, she has a poem in issue fifteen of *Tiferet*.

As for the idea of an informing vision, the very words you use in the question—"all-encompassing" and "informing vision"—these words feel, to me, very akin to oneness. And this oneness, or unity, is core to my vision of reality. In other words, I see people, myself included, as individual vehicles or vessels, each of us with unique gifts and capacities, and each of us with our own journeys. Yet, we're extraordinarily intertwined and interconnected: a sort of web or ocean or tapestry of oneness. That's just how I see the world. I can't choose to see it in another way—that wouldn't feel true. That would feel like jettisoning one of my gifts.

When I think about this informing vision, this oneness, I actually think about the painters Van Gogh and Matisse, whose works really depicted the vibrational and unified nature of reality. The Van Gogh painting I particularly think of is *The Starry Night*. Do you know the one I am talking about?

MELISSA: Yes, I love that painting.

JUDE: So many people do, and there are people who actually see that way, who

The truth of one's experience is an enormous thing.

see things vibrating in the way that painting depicts. I imagine he had this gift, which also would be, in many ways, a curse at that time. So, he conveyed his truth, and that's what I try to do, too. I try to convey the truth of my experience. The truth of one's experience is an enormous thing.

Not being able to look away from the truth of one's experience can be an extraordinary gift and also a great curse at times. I think Van Gogh was a testament to that. When the majority of the world can't see reality the way it is, the truth-seers, the truth-tellers, can feel painfully disconnected, separate, outside, rejected, unreceived. Actually, this is the oldest punishment known to humans. The punishment that was used in ancient times was ostracism—putting one outside of the community.

MELISSA: I thought for a minute you were going to say that being an artist was the oldest punishment known to humans.

JUDE: No, no, no, no, no. Putting someone outside of community was a way to punish them, and, I'm sure, to keep the community safe. But, that concept of being on the outside is also what the word "sin" is about. The word "sin" actually comes from the Latin word "sine," which means "without." So, think about that: sin, being separate from All That Is. That is the human paradox. We feel separate from, yet we are a part of that great oneness. And it's really difficult to hold the awareness that those things are simultaneously true. So, to answer your question, paradoxical truth—that's what my informing vision is.

MELISSA: Will you read some excerpts from your long poem "The Languages of Light," which runs from pages 69 to 76 in issue fifteen of Tiferet?

JUDE: Here are parts of the poem. It's in sections, so I'll identify the sections as I read.

> The Languages of Light
> I
> Words alone are tired foot soldiers.
> Let me speak to you through moon,
> hanging lonely above Orion's circuit.
>
> Moon, too, always circling: following earth
> like a steadfast consort. Does moon notice
> Orion's fruitless chase?
>
> Those seven sisters racing,
> forever out of his reach. Spurning him.
> Needing only the broad arms
>
> of each other's light. Poor Orion, his
> points of light separated by such wide darkness.
> Wide to my eyes—seeing all this from earth

as she spins her dance of needing sun,
though she dare not touch him. Can you hear
my kindred longing? Moon, stars, earth

showing me how it's done: this hunger
for what I need but cannot touch.
Weary words: unwashed, unshaven, growing

hopeless. Though they once believed
in their bootless mission: bringing the world,
by force, to peace. But I am a small country

and words are what I have
to slog through the quagmires, fields
and shifting sands—the continents between us.

The lands which keep our waters
from touching. Prevent us
from flowing together in a bottomless dance.

Instead of words, imagine we share a bed
on Prince Edward Island at Dalvay by the Sea.
A full moon lifts herself

above the Northumberland Straits. She trails
her light the way I rise over you: my body
emulating moon on mirror waves. Rising, falling.

Undulating. Coming
as close as humans can without words.
Afterwards, beyond sun's first light and waking,

the thirst remains
for what words can never convey.
Think of those ravenous families of stars out there

with no other arms but their light.
Think how sun's rays mate with ocean
each clear morning. We have no word

for this ritual, this shining. We have only skin
longing to feel a dance like that
filling it from shore to shore.

II
Having forgotten
this particular dialect of light,
we humans speak

in glints, glances, glares, aversions
learned from parents, teachers, elders
whose eyes shaped us.

Wrote the encyclopedia
of our bodies, our lives
with a limited vocabulary

edited and bound by their acceptable terms.
Mutely, dumbly they defined us
with warm or icy visages that said:

Yes, more of that obedient
silence, that perfect sweet smile. No,
make those fists and tears disappear.

XIV
Imagine knowing your heart like earth
knows its meadows. Like a stargazer
lily convinced by its scent, a daisy its petals,

forsythia its yellow, the milkweed pod
each feathered seed. Let me know
myself like a rose knows red.

XVI
We may rewrite
our chasms of silencings,
sensing cobwebbed

dust-infested libraries
inside us.
Entire wings filled with manuals

on multifarious ways of being.
Lexicons never opened. Never even
shown to us. Ineffable volumes,

like ocean, speaking about deepening.
Showing us how to bask, how to dance
tangos, waltzes, jitterbugs, even

the sacred whirl of a dervish.
Or primers like sunlight. Yes, sun
whirling July into August.

Hot light tiring of itself. Diminishing

a bit more each day. Darkness
laying down thicker, heavier blankets.

Insulating us. Swaddling us. Waiting
for us to find what smolders inside.
Waiting for us to feed our flames.

XVII
Even without skin,
Polaris, the North Star, reflects
in No Bottom Pond

stretching its lanky body
on Hidden Valley's belly.
These connected essences

press against the chest
of Bared Breast Mountain.
Yet not one of these

reached out arms,
star to mountain to valley to pond,
longing to hold someone

intimately. Light penetrating water,
water caressing valley,
valley pressing itself

upon up-thrusting stone. Don't trust me
to tell you the truth here. Listen, instead,
to your own body

as it speaks about such things. Notice
how your legs, even now,
huddle together like lonely soldiers

and your throat reaches down as if to pull
the answer
from your heart. Asking for a response

like light asking water asking dirt asking rock:
Who are we,
all of us together in the cold?

XVIII
Light can be terribly
patient. After all it's been through,
what's a year or decade or century or eon

to a particle of light? Nothing
but momentum. Nothing but a journey:
continuity, transformation. Nothing but a dervish dance.

MELISSA: That was a beautiful reading. You've said in the past that this particular poem is near and dear to your heart. Would you elaborate on what it is that sets this poem apart from the others for you?

JUDE: I rarely write anything longer than a couple of pages, and this poem is long. It kind of blew me away to have that happen—to have that develop.

MELISSA: I remember seeing that the first section of this poem is actually presented as its own poem in your earlier chapbook. When and how did you realize that this first section was actually part of a larger poem?

JUDE: It's akin to what I was saying about individuality and unity: the paradox of two things—seemingly separate or even opposites— that are actually true and necessary to each other. In the same vein, there are two sections, and possibly even three, in this long poem that can also work as stand-alone, individual poems. In fact, they were originally elsewhere on their own or as parts of another poem.

When I started this sequence, it was called, "Words Without Words," and I was drawn into a sense of trying to put words to images and ideas that really are larger than words. After I completed that sequence and let it sit for a while—let it become what it wanted to become and let it reveal itself to me—a moment came when I said, "Oh, this poem belongs in the beginning, and this poem is the ending." So, it fell together like that, and it was a process, something that took place over a long period of time.

MELISSA: Do you mind if I ask how long?

JUDE: I'm really hard-pressed to answer that because I know I wrote the final section five to ten years back, in the sequence that was "Words without Words." I think I completed that sequence a couple of years ago. I don't even remember

I have to be willing to go into the creative act having no idea what's going to come of it. The delight, pleasure, and joy of the creative act is not knowing, abiding in the total unknown, allowing the swirl of chaos and creation to come in and fill the form.

when I wrote "Living in Skin." I'd originally called it "Even Without Skin." Living in a land of non-linearity, not focusing on or remembering the sequence of the process, is one of the challenges and gifts of writing.

Burghild Nina Holzer wrote a beautiful journal on the creative process called *A Walk Between Heaven and Earth*. One of her pieces of advice is that you have to be willing to let something sit for a long while, until you get "used to its strangeness or its embarrassment." The way I would put that is: I have to be willing to go into the creative act having no idea what's going to come of it. The delight, pleasure, and joy of the creative act is not knowing, abiding in the total unknown, allowing the swirl of chaos and creation to come in and fill the form. In the case of writing, that form takes shape as words on the page.

I engage with other creative practices so that when words aren't coming I'm using another creative form. I find that one art feeds another. I often have many projects going on at the same time, and I sometimes discover: "Oh, wow, it's all of a piece." Then later, sometimes much later, it reveals to me what I was just beginning to glimpse. And it actually teaches me what I'm ready to know.

MELISSA: I think you really touched on something interesting about having to be patient—not only with the creative process, but with the work itself—to let it gestate and turn into what it needs to be. I hadn't realized the connection before, but when you were talking about that, I was thinking of Whitman and *Leaves of Grass*, as I'm sure many listeners were—about how he worked on that for a lifetime, really. And I heard some echoes of Keats and was reminded of

Rilke too. Were any of these writers major influences for you? If not, who was?

JUDE: Rilke, of course; he's just so inspiring. *Letters to a Young Poet* was very influential for me. At some point, when I was in my late twenties or early thirties, I realized that I had spent my entire life up to that point reading primarily male authors, because when I was young, that's what schools taught. I was a voracious reader, and I was also an English major in both high school and college for my undergraduate degree.

When I realized this discrepancy, I made a conscious decision to spend an equivalent amount of time focused on female writers, and I have really fulfilled that obligation—that rebalancing. Now I am back into reading a mix and enjoying it. I remember falling in love at age fifteen with Muriel Rukeyser's poem "Effort at Speech Between Two People." Do you know that poem?

MELISSA: No, but I do know much of her work, and I can tell from the title how in sync that is with your subject matter.

JUDE: Yes, she really had her fingers on the pulse of human longing. Of course, there's Emily Dickinson too. And I feel like I have been as much influenced not just by poets but also by novelists, playwrights, nonfiction writers, and science fiction writers.

Doris Lessing: she's a phenomenal writer, and I'm so glad she finally won the Nobel Prize in literature. I particularly loved her space fiction series. Fyodor Dostoevsky—I really went through a Russian phase. Then Ursula Le Guin, who writes gorgeous fantasy/science fiction. Tennessee Williams, James Agee, Heinrich Böll, Virginia Woolf, Nikolai Gogol. Eugene O'Neill: I went through a phase where I read everything I could get my hands on by O'Neill; then, once I finished all of his writing, I moved onto everything I could get my hands on about him. I read all of his major biographies.

Marge Piercy, a contemporary writer, was a major early influence. I loved *Woman on the Edge of Time*; that novel moved me deeply, as did much of her poetry. Faulkner: I went through a real Faulkner phase and stayed entrenched in his novels for quite a while early in my life. Oriana Fallaci: an absolutely stunning nonfiction writer, who also wrote two novels: *A Man* and *Inshallah*. Vladimir Nabokov, Rumi, (Coleman Bark's translations of Rumi), Richard Feynman, and other authors like him, who helped me to understand physics. And, then, of course, contemporary poets like Sharon Olds, Mary Oliver, Ruth Stone—a wonderful woman. Li-Young Lee, Tony Hoagland, and, of course, Lucille Clifton. William Meredith and Gwendolyn Brooks, who have passed. Those are just some of them.

I think my earliest influences were probably Ogden Nash and Edgar Allen Poe. That's a weird combination, but my father loved both. He was hardly ever home, but occasionally—on very special occasions, he would do a performance for the youngest three or four of us from Nash's "Custard the Dragon."

My father also loved and would sometimes recite Poe's poem "Annabel Lee." He had two copies of Poe—one soft leather bound, one hard leather bound—and I usurped one of them. I consumed every word of it when I was prepubescent, I think. I started writing before kindergarten because I started reading before kindergarten. I had a wonderful older sister—she is an amazing woman—who taught me to read and write before I started school. I think I probably wrote my first poem between the ages of four and six and wrote a really bad science fiction mystery when I was about eleven.

MELISSA: That sounds like a wonderful literary heritage. I understand you're developing a teleconference series called "Women in Metamorphosis." Can you tell us more about that?

JUDE: We don't have specific dates yet, but there will be information about it on the Tiferet Journal website once we get the details in place. So here's what I know about it thus far. We are in such a transitional time right now. Everyone I know is going through major transformations, and I think those of us who are in our middle and later years are feeling like we are recreating ourselves yet again. It can seem a little daunting, so I think people need a community to support them.

"Women in Metamorphosis" will be the title because that's what I know about. I hope a man will do a workshop on men in metamorphosis because I think we all need people who understand us to help support us through these times.

The series will be somewhere between four and six sessions in a teleconference call. We are going to create a very safe and sacred place where we can explore who we have been, who we are, and what our lives are asking of us now, including what we have to be willing to release. That's often the hardest part.

We are going to enter in to that large territory of unknowns that always wait for each of us, and we will open ourselves to whatever is there, calling for our attention, waiting to come through us as the next creation. In the process of working together, we will make sure that we are honoring each other by receiving anything that surfaces in a very conscious and sacred way, sharing our stories and our journeys as we go.

I think of Muriel Rukeyser's lines from the poem "Käthe Kollwitz": "What would happen if one woman told / the truth about her life? / The world would split open..." I think that's really, in a way, what's happening right now. More and more people are telling the truth about their lives, and the world is splitting open. It's transforming.

I will read to you what I have in the way of a blurb for this series of workshops: "Throughout our lives, our bodies have taught us life's greatest truth over and over again: The nature of life and creation is change. Now, as our bodies, our society and our lives change once again, we may struggle with the seemingly limited range of choices and opportunities, forgetting that we have each grown amazing wisdom about what is needed. This series of workshops will support us, and we will support each other as we explore what we know, what we must let go of, what we don't know, and what we long to create in our lives as we transform the fecund loam of our former selves into brilliant future gardens."

MELISSA: This seems like a good place to ask you some questions about your nondual healing practice. I know it goes by several different names, which could be confusing to some people. Could you explain those a little bit and also what the process is, as much as you can?

JUDE: My practice is called Integrated Healing Services, and you can find that website at www.integratedhealingservices.com to learn more.

Anything that can be put into words is not going to be what the experience is; you can only get it from the experience itself

My primary modality is Nondual Kabbalistic Healing (NKH) ®. That's also known as Integrated Kabbalistic Healing (IKH).

This work is hard to put into words. The reason for that is similar to what many people have heard as an explanation about Taoism and The Way in Taoism: if you can describe The Way, it's not the true way. In my twenties, I used to really mull over that phrase and think: What does that mean? I understand what it means now. Anything that can be put into words is not going to be what the experience is; you can only get it from the experience itself. I would say that same thing is true about Nondual Kabbalistic Healing®. Any words I might say about it will be such an understatement. It's an ineffable, enormous and transformative process.

Having said that, I'll try to give something of a definition; just know that what I can put into words is going to be far less than what actually takes place. This nondual practice finds the common ground in Kabbalah, Buddhism, psychology, physics and so many wisdom traditions. Truth is found in that common ground. NKH® utilizes the Tree of Life, which is a symbol—part of the kabbalistic field—and draws on awarenesses about the kabbalistic universes.

NKH® uses the elements of creation and aspects of divinity embodied in The Tree of Life; this healing work gently rectifies our longings for connection, a sense of place and a sense of victory: the qualities that help us feel grounded, safe, successful, worthy. It also rebalances our relationship with order and chaos, so that we gain an increasing ability to navigate life's ever-changing territory of old structures dissolving to make way for new creations. It helps stretch our capacity to receive and be received: to be with all that is. So our relationship to life itself changes as we come to deeply know our place—our home in the scheme of things. Organically, like seeds slowly growing into trees, who dance with earth-rain-sky, we discover that our separateness was also made to stretch and relax into spacious unity.

When we practice Nondual Kabbalistic Healing®, we're using all of this and we're also coming from an intensive training, a four-year process that is very transformational for those who have been through it. You change throughout the course of those years and become a very different container. You develop an ability to receive people in a way that's quite extraordinary. In fact, receiving—from the kabbalistic perspective—is very foundational. And, when you think about it, receiving is a foundational thing about reality: receiving and being received. Relationship is the foundation of everything. It's simply what's going on all the time. Physicists know that everything is in relationship and changing constantly because of the relational nature of reality. So, Nondual Kabbalistic Healing® is an extremely kind and compassionate way to receive and reconnect with whatever has split off—become fragmented or disconnected—and bring it back into harmony, unity, wholeness.

Is there anything that I've left muddy or that requires further clarification?

MELISSA: I can't think of anything, but I would like to remind people that they can call in, so if there's anything that anyone would like clarified, they are welcome to ask, or they are welcome to call in with other questions as well.

I do have another question to follow up on that. Do you think spiritual practice is important to an artist's life, and, as well, do you think artistic creation enhances spiritual practice?

JUDE: That's an interesting question particularly because it presumes that there's some kind of a separation between art and spirituality or between spirituality and anything. To me, such separation is a false thing—an illusion. I think this is an awareness that I gained in the Nondual Kabbalistic Healing training®: it's all one thing.

To me, art is a spiritual practice, and I think I didn't even realize for many decades that creativity was my primary spiritual practice. Writing was my spiritual practice. Art is a way of looking at the world, trying to really see it, trying to understand something about it and then conveying what we glimpse along the way. To me, writing itself is a journey, and, I think I mentioned earlier, I often don't have any idea what I'm going to write about when I begin. The process itself guides me, leads me, informs me, teaches me, and I can't separate spiritual practice from art or vice versa. To separate those things feels as false as any other separation. Living is a spiritual practice.

MELISSA: Do you have any advice for someone who might want to bring their life into the kind of balance you have found with your creativity, spirituality, and writing? I can also tell from reading your poems and blogs that the way you interact with the natural world and with other people is cohesive and connected to your practices of writing and art. It reminds me of something one of my professors, Marie Howe, used to say. It

The process itself guides me, leads me, informs me, teaches me, and I can't separate spiritual practice from art or vice versa. To separate those things feels as false as any other separation. Living is a spiritual practice.

was something her professor, Stanley Kunitz, said to her—that in order to write the kind of poems you want to write you should start by becoming the kind of person who would write those poems.

JUDE: That's so beautiful.

MELISSA: Isn't it wonderful? And, actually, it reminds me of you. To me, you are the perfect example of that, so do you have advice for other people who would like to bring their lives into that kind of balance?

JUDE: I feel very honored that you see me as a person who is living life like that. I try. We all try. But, we also don't always know if we are succeeding. I think that, for me, achieving balance and becoming who I want to be in life starts with self-kindness, self-compassion. And that's been a really hard thing for me to learn, because I grew up in a family that was extraordinarily critical and judgmental, and I think they didn't know that. It wasn't done with any intent to harm. It was, if anything, done with an intention of protecting. So, I've had to really learn—and I will spend the rest of my life working to learn—to be compassionate and kind. First to myself, in order to be that way with others.

That, I think, is a beginning point. Other pieces are: being willing to explore the dark places in one's self and being willing to make those places transparent, because that's where light comes from. Going in, diving deep, and finding what's there, then mining it—that's where the powerful material comes from. Without that, what you've got is somebody else's stuff, somebody else's version of the world. Learning to come from the inside out, instead of the outside in, is primary when one wants to live a centered life, when one wants to create art. Do you know Natalie Goldberg's rules of writing?

MELISSA: Absolutely.

JUDE: She says that those rules are equally applicable to life in general. I'd say that's because creating art and creating a life that one can feel really good about, or even just bear to lead, comes from the same place: the place that longs for truth, longs to live in increasingly conscious and connected ways. Learning how to do that can begin when you begin to connect with yourself—your truth—and come from the inside out, instead of trying to live the way you think the world wants you to be.

MELISSA: That's very helpful. I want to shift and ask you about some of the recurring images and patterns in your work. Obviously, images such as the ocean, water, the moon, and trees recur. I'm sure people heard this when you read the excerpts from "The Languages of Light." I noticed an elements image pattern in your poems—air, fire, water, and earth—as well. Is this a conscious technique on your part?

JUDE: It's both conscious and unconscious, I suppose. Nature just feels like as much a part of my family as my parents, my sister, or my brothers do. I think, when I was small, nature sometimes felt like a safer part of my family—trees, particularly. I have such a thing for trees—maples, especially. Trees, sky, clouds, wind, earth, light—these natural things, even when I couldn't go out and be in them, even if they were just in my head—they gave me an escape. They were places to go in my mind when I was little and having difficulty being in physical proximity to the energies and the people around me.

Later, when I learned about Jung, and archetypal images and the collective unconscious, I began to recognize that the appeal and power these things had for me was universal. It's like using a tuning fork when one evokes these images: it's like playing a note and things start to resonate at that same vibration, because they have similar qualities. So, for me this natural resonance is just what's there. It's just what is. Nature is very large in my experience and in my life. I hope that answers your question.

MELISSA: Yes—it does. Your writing, I think, takes the idea of pathetic fallacy to a whole new level, where human action and thought isn't just mirrored by nature but is actually a part of nature. Humans are not distinguished from the landscape any more than a tree or a squirrel. So, what you're saying makes a great deal of sense in that context. Now, you also talk a lot about what it means to be human. The journey of being human is one of the primary subjects in your blog and your poems. Can you talk about that?

JUDE: First, I want to say something about the words "pathetic fallacy," because those who are immersed in the world of literature and literary criticism know what that phrase means, but, to people who don't know what the phrase means, it may feel like pathetic fallacy has negative or pejorative connotations.

MELISSA: Yes. You're right. Please go ahead.

JUDE: What we're talking about—pathetic fallacy—is something that goes beyond anthropomorphism and personification. To me, what we're talking about is simply what is. We humans tend to be so homocentric. It's not that I'm viewing nature with human qualities; it's that I can't help but feel, and notice, and see all of the aliveness and sentience in nature.

You asked a question about what it means to be human. Being human means that we are in material form, and that, in and of itself, means we are vulnerable. It means that we are able to experience great joy and also tremendous pain.

A little over a year ago, I almost died after contracting three tick-borne diseases. The various diseases destroyed my blood, which stressed my heart. My kidneys were shutting down, my organs were shutting down, and while I was at death's threshold, I had this amazing experience of floating in a timeless, black, waterless sea. Suspended there with me were the eyes of whales and elephants—ancient eyes that conveyed a divine sadness, a heartbreak that humans haven't become the stewards of earth that we were meant to become.

We humans think that we are masters of creation. We are not. We try to control things in this world, and over and over we are shown that we have no control. Everything can disappear in an instant. That's a lesson I learned deeply a year ago, and it's a lesson I feel so keenly these days as I watch many people struggling with the enormous changes that are happening in their lives and in the world: social, economic, environmental and political changes that hugely impact individuals as well as their communities and societies.

We live in times that require increasing levels of creativity and flexibility, as well as enormous compassion. Many in the aging population of this country have watched economic crashes and escalating healthcare costs eradicate plans and options for their final decades. Families have lost their homes. Meanwhile, we continue to be exposed to increasing levels of violence via movies and games, as well as through acts of terrorism and through nature's wild eruptions and upheavals. Here and all over the world, changes seem to be happening quickly. Also, the desperation that people live with seems to be getting louder, whether or not it is. If it is, maybe the increasing noise will help us to hear and respond with kindness toward ourselves, each other, the planet—with compassion toward all that is.

Being human means being in form, thus being vulnerable to enormous changes. And because we have bodies, we have preferences. I don't know anyone who doesn't prefer comfort over pain. We all want to be comfortable. Nobody likes pain, and because we have preferences, we grow attached to people, places, things, even comfort itself. We live in a society that prefers youth over age, thinness over plumpness, wealth over poverty.

So, being human means struggling, and because we all struggle, we might also have immense and enormous compassion for each other. I think life's losses are meant to bring us into com- passion for other people. Things don't always play out that way, but I really feel like that's what these enor-

Being human means being in form, thus being vulnerable to enormous changes. And because we have bodies, we have preferences.

mously transforming times are calling us to do: to recognize that we are all vulnerable to losing everything at any moment.

A line that keeps coming to me these days is, "In order to gain everything, we must first lose or let go of everything." Really, that's what's required of us when we are in material form. Mat- ter constantly changes, and—no matter what crazy things we humans do to avoid knowing it—that's the truth of being human. We are in material form. Loss is a part of things. Gain is a part of loss. This is the way the world works. So, I guess my life-goal and my intention on this journey of being human is to open my heart and release any negative judgments and criticisms, know- ing that these are simply ways of trying to protect myself from pain and loss. Even though it's hard to be open and vulnerable, it's stultifying, brittle and fragile to be closed: it provides only a small and temporary sense of protection and safety. It feels so true to me that in order to gain everything we must lose every- thing. And it feels terribly challenging to actually do that—to let go. Seeing this, knowing this, how can we not have compassion for each other?

MELISSA: That's a great answer. I'm noticing that we only have about five minutes left, and we have a caller, so I'm going to let the caller through, and then we'll wind things down.

CALLER: Hi. This is Diane from Massachusetts. I just wanted to ask Jude about that critical voice which she mentions. I think many of us suffer that when we try to write. Can she give any suggestions for trying to quiet that critical voice?

JUDE: I can suggest a marvelous book. It's called *Soul without Shame*, by Byron Brown. Tara Brach's *Radical Acceptance* is also inspiring and helpful.

Also, I think that self-kindness is a daily, moment by moment practice, and the only way to do it is to simply do it. It can begin by noticing every time you say the word *should*, because should is a judgment word, and it's a subtle one. If you really let yourself feel your body when you hear yourself using that word, notice how you tend to curl inward a little bit in self-protection. There are so many subtle and small ways that we judge ourselves. If you want to get the inner critic to stop judging your writing, you have to get it to stop judging your life in general.

CALLER: Excellent. Thank you so much.

MELISSA: I have to say I didn't get to half of what I wanted to ask, so maybe you can come back sometime, and we can talk more.

JUDE: Certainly. It has been a pleasure. Thank you so much.

Photograph by Julie Dermansky

EDWARD HIRSCH

OCTOBER 14, 2010

MELISSA: Our interview tonight is with Edward Hirsch—poet, editor, professor and Guggenheim Foundation president. Hirsch is the author of eight books of poems as well as the best-selling book, How to Read a Poem and Fall in Love with Poetry. His numerous awards include a National Book Critics Circle Award and the MacArthur Foundation Fellowship. A tireless advocate for the importance of poetry, Hirsch has stated, "I am convinced the kind of experience—the kind of knowledge—one gets from poetry cannot be duplicated elsewhere. The spiritual life wants articulation—it wants embodiment in language. The physical life wants the spirit. I know this because I hear it in the words, because when I liberate the message in the bottle—a physical—a spiritual urgency pulses through the arranged text. It is as if the spirit grows in my hands. Or the words rise in the air. 'Roots and wings,' the Spanish poet Juan Ramón Jiménez writes, 'but let the wings take root and the roots fly.' "

Ed, I'm going to jump right in and ask you a huge question to start. Based on the quote I just read and on the statement you make in Poet's Choice—that poetry is a human fundamental like music—can you talk about your views regarding the purpose of poetry for humanity and also the role of the poet in society, particularly in contemporary American society?

ED: Well, that is a large question. I can't get to the bottom of this in a few minutes, but let me take a shot. Maybe we can break it down into two parts. First: the role of poetry as a human fundamental, and, then—the role of poetry in America.

First of all, the evidence: There's never been a culture without poetry. That's why I call it a human fundamental. Poetry exists everywhere. There's language in every culture. So, this makes me think that people write poetry and read or listen to poetry not just because they are some particularly aesthetic-minded or weird people who like it, like you and me. It's not just that there are some bohemians who like poetry, even though there are some bohemians who care for it. It's that poetry has been instrumental to the making of culture all around the world. This makes me think there must be something necessary in poetry.

Now, I'm not saying it's the same thing that's necessary in every culture or to every poet or that every person who goes to poetry seeks the same thing. But the fact that there is poetry and that it came to be is not accidental. That is, poetry must be carrying some kind of information, some kind of knowledge that we are not getting elsewhere. Because, after all, poems are difficult. And, so, if it would be easier to get it somewhere else we just would. We'd just turn on the TV or turn on the radio or put on our iPhone or whatever. Wherever we are, we have other kinds of entertainment.

But this kind of entertainment, this kind of fiction-making seems really crucial to human beings and so the question is: What is that? And, in different cultures, I think it means different things. Traditionally, in all oral cultures, there are epics that are narrative stories that tell the tale of the tribe. And this is absolutely fundamental to people's understanding of themselves in oral cultures. So, poets are kind of the cultural historians and myth makers of a culture. They tell you the story of the culture of what it means to be Yorba or what it means to be Slovakian or whatever. It tells you what it means to be part of a tribe, to be part of a culture. For those of us living in non-tribal cultures, poetry offers us, I think, a kind of, I would say, unauthorized testimony. The overlap with religion is a gray area, but the difference is that religion is authorized. It comes with the cultural power and spiritual authority of a group or a church, whatever that church is. And people who join the church subscribe in certain ways to the doctrine of the church.

In poetry, there is no church. But, there is spiritual testimony, and that's why I call it unauthorized testimony. It's necessary as a spiritual testament, but it comes from a single person, from one without the authority of the group. It comes from the authority of the individual. That seems to me to be very American, very necessary for us, because of our great tradition of individuality, of the individual testament. Is this making sense to you?

MELISSA: Absolutely. I especially like the way you took it in a historical direction because I wanted to see how you would trace it back. So, thank you. I'd like to ask you about something a little more esoteric from one of your books, and I hope you remember writing about it because you have so many books. I've studied the creative process quite a bit, and when I read about your theories on lucid delirium, I was especially interested in your analogy between articulate creation and shamanism. Could you explain the analogy for the listeners, and maybe even share the insights you have about the creative process?

ED: I suspect you are thinking about *The Demon and the Angel*. Is that what you're talking about? Because that book tries to think about the subject of our artistic inspiration and what's involved in artistic inspiration. And poetry, as Freud thought, is akin to daydreaming. It has a relationship to dreams as well as to daydreaming, but it's consciously made and unconsciously driven.

The reason I called it a lucid delirium is because it's not just delirious thinking—it's not just random irrationality, but it does tap some of the fevers and the powers of the irrational, the unconscious. Creative inspiration is something that comes from deep inside of us—a well of creating something new, something that drives up from inside of us to put something new in the world. The need is some combination of conscious thought and unconscious power. And the unconscious power is the element of the irrational or the delirious.

The shaman is a kind of priest figure who becomes the stand-in for this kind of knowledge and who delivers this kind of information. There's a terrific book by Mircea Eliade on shamanism around the world. In it, he shows the power of shamanism in oral cultures everywhere in the world, and there's no doubt that the shaman is a kind of poet in many oral cultures. But the difference is that in these cultures, the poet is also a priest. And the shaman has certain ritual functions, ritual things to do in bringing forward the oral religion and remembering the rites of a particular tribe.

So, our poets are not priests, but they have certain priestly functions, or they carry certain weight, certain kinds of information, certain kinds of knowledge that poets have always carried. That's why I compare them to shamans who know how to consciously put themselves into trances.

MELISSA: I've never heard that analogy before, and to me it's so poignant about what actually happens in the creative process and in the bringing back.

ED: This is why it's so dangerous and so difficult. Because, you know, you are in dangerous territory. You are in deep waters.

MELISSA: I couldn't agree more. As you were talking about that, I was thinking that one of the things I love about your poetry is that you've got such an amazing balance between magic and craft, which, of course, relates to what we're talking about. Is there any advice you could give to other writers or other artists about how they can balance craft and inspiration?

ED: Well, this is complicated. And if we knew how to bottle it, then we not only would be great teachers, but we'd have a lot more great artists. So, it's very hard to figure this out, but I think you're pointing to something that's important to me in terms of the practice of art, and that is that there's no authentic art, in my opinion, without this magical, irrational, unconscious element. It is something that is unpremeditated and something deeply spiritual. And, when we read poems, when we write poems, when we look at paintings, when we listen to certain pieces of music, we feel this being delivered to ourselves.

At the same time, I don't believe that art is entirely unconscious. I think you have to somehow put yourself in the presence of this

> *One thing about writing poetry is that you can't just walk around waiting for inspiration. You can have a very long wait.*

spirit, but it also has to be delivered formally. I think many poets let themselves down and let others down as well because they just don't learn enough about their craft. Everything that can be learned about your craft should be learned. There's a tremendous amount that you can teach yourself in the practice of any craft—whether it's poetry, fiction, the making of music, or the making of art of any sort. And, so, it is part of your job description to learn about your art and to work in an apprenticeship to make yourself the best artist that you can be.

Now, that being said, I think it also is useful to know, and to remember, that conscious work itself—conscious labor—is not entirely sufficient. In his great defense of poetry, Shelly says, "not even the greatest poet can say 'I will write poetry.'" There's always something inexplicable, something outside the conscious control of the poet in the writing of authentic poetry. That's why poets are so superstitious. That's why poets call on so many forces beyond themselves.

So, whenever you hear about an ancient poet calling, "help me, oh heavenly muse," what is he calling on? What is he calling for? And, whatever you want to call that, whether you call it *the muse*, or you want to call it *creativity*, or you want to call it, as Jung does, the *collective unconscious*, or you want to call it the *unconscious*, as Freud does, or the *uncanny* or the "White Goddess" as Robert Graves does, whatever name you give to it, it's doing the same thing. It's recognizing that there is a power, whether it is outside ourselves or inside ourselves—as I believe—that must be summoned or that you hope to summon, in the creation of art. And that's the element of magic. So, you try to put yourself in the way of that magic.

MELISSA: You've said before that the creation of poetry is messy and that when you're coming to a poem and about to create a poem, you never know exactly how it will happen. Sometimes it's an image, sometimes it's a voice, sometimes it's a story that you want to tell. Can you elaborate on that and tell us if there are any constants in the mess, and, if so, what they are?

ED: One thing about writing poetry is that you can't just walk around waiting for inspiration. You can have a very long wait. Randall Jarrell (wrote), "A good poet is someone who manages, in a lifetime of standing out in thunderstorms, to be struck by lightning five or six times; a dozen or two dozen times and he is great."

You can't be sure you'll get hit by lighting, but you need to go out and stand in the rain, or you won't get hit at all. You need to do your work. So, one of the constants is that you need to fasten your behind in the chair and sit down and do some work and try to consciously practice your craft. Now, the reason I think the writing of poetry is messy is because you don't know exactly what you're going to get or how you're going to get there. Sometimes you begin with a formal idea, sometimes you begin with something you need to write about, sometimes you begin with the sound of certain words, sometimes you begin with something you read in another poem that you want to try. And then you start going to work on your poem.

Now, the constant, I would say, is, "What does it take for me to write a poem that I think is good or that I can live with?" For me there are two parts to this. One: Something important has to be at stake. There has to be something really meaningful to me that gets down to where I really live in my unconscious. So, something has to be a risk. And then, something has to happen formally. I myself just can't write a poem without some formal idea, some formal recognition. It doesn't have to be a traditional form, but there has to be some shape, something has to come forward and present itself that I can shape and turn into something. You know the oldest word in Greek for poetry is "poiesis," which means, "making," and I hold fast to the idea that a poet is a maker and a poem is a made thing. So, you have to make something. And, so, you have to figure out how to do that, and, for me, one of the constants is that I have to have some formal idea at some point in the writing of the poem, not always at the beginning, but something has to kick in to try and create a structure.

MELISSA: Is there typically a certain point where you recognize what kind of beast you are actually dealing with?

ED: Yes, there's a certain point where you go, "This is it." The process is kind of mysterious because you're trying to lead, but you're also following. But at a certain point, you need to say, "I'm going to make this a song, or I'm going to make this into three line stanzas, or I'm going to use a dropped line, or I'm going to extend this metaphor," and you can't just let it happen. You have to harness it, and, so, as you begin to harness it, you begin to see it deployed. I mean, in a certain way, a poem is like a piece of music. It's got a structure and it sets up expectations which are fulfilled or thwarted or turned. William Carlos Williams said, "A poem is a small (or large) machine made out of words." There's nothing redundant about a machine. So, at a certain point you need to figure out how you are going to make that machine, and sometimes you begin with the idea of how you are going to make it, and sometimes you discover it as you go.

MELISSA: When you finish writing a poem, do you know pretty quickly whether you've written a good poem, or does it take a while?

ED: I think you feel ecstatic after you finish a poem—at least I do— and I think it's really great. Or, it still continues to bother you, and then you know it's not really finished. But, after it settles for a couple of days or a little while, sometimes you see what you thought

> *Whatever accomplishments or whatever you have, that's not going to save you from the difficulty of having to write the next poem. You're always a beginner in some way.*

was great maybe isn't so great after all, and the excitement that you feel in finishing something isn't necessarily a guide to how lasting it's going to be. So, you can be wildly excited about something and find out that actually it doesn't work at all. Other times, you can be a little less ecstatic because you couldn't quite get it the way you wanted it, and then you find out it has got something that really seems to stick. So, you are not really a good judge of your own work when you are in the very frenzy of working it and completing it. That takes a colder eye at some later point.

MELISSA: It's interesting to hear someone as far along and as accomplished as you still saying that.

ED: Whatever accomplishments or whatever you have, that's not going to save you from the difficulty of having to write the next poem. You're always a beginner in some way. You're always starting out, and you always bring that frame of mind—because I think you need to be humble for the process, because you are not entirely in control of it. You're just doing your best.

MELISSA: Could you read a few poems for us?

ED: That would be my pleasure. Why don't I start out with "A Chinese Vase."

A Chinese Vase

Sometimes I think that my body is a vase
With me in it, a blue-tiled Chinese vase

That I return to sometimes in the rain.
It's raining hard, but inside the little china vase

There is clean white water circling slowly
Through the shadows like a flock of yellow geese

Circling over a small lake, or like the lake itself
Ruffled with wind and geese in a light rain

That is not dirty, or stained, or even ruffled by
The medley of motors and oars and sometimes even sails

That are washed each summer to her knees. It's raining
In the deep poplars and in the stand of gray pines;

It's snowing in the mountains, in the Urals, in the
Wastes of Russia that have edged off into China;

The rain has turned to sleet and the sleet
Has turned to snow in the sullen black clouds

That have surfaced in the cracks of that Chinese
Vase, in the wrinkles that have widened like rivers

In that vase of china. It's snowing harder and harder
Now over the mountains, but inside the mountains

There is a sunlit cave, a small cave, perhaps,
Like a monk's cell, or like a small pond

With geese and with clear mountain water inside.
Sometimes I think that I come back to my body

The way a penitent or a pilgrim or a poet
Or a whore or a murderer or a very young girl

Comes for the first time to a holy place
To kneel down, to forget the impossible weight

Of being human, to drink clear water.

MELISSA: That was beautiful. I love that poem.

ED: It goes off on a lot of wild flights.

MELISSA: It does, it does! I want to ask you about that, because I was reading your theories about metamorphosis and transformation, and in that poem the body is a vase, and the vase is a world; then the cave is the monk's cell, and then a pond with geese. The whole thing is a swirl of movement and transformation. We were just talking about how the process is different with each poem. What was it like to create that poem? Was there anything magical in that?

ED: The whole poem moves as a metaphor. "My body is a vase with me in it." Now, that's a weird analogy right there. I mean it's peculiar.

MELISSA: It is a wonderful, weird analogy.

ED: I liked it, and I wondered, "What happens if you push this? Let's see—let's take this thinking and see how far we can go with it." The metaphysical poets, whom I greatly admire, loved to work with what Samuel Johnson called a "conceit," or a form of wit. The idea is to take a metaphor and push it as far as possible. Now, in every metaphor there's a contradiction. It always breaks down because you say one thing is something else. A is B. And of course, two things are not the same, so the metaphor will always break down at a certain point. So the question is: How far can you push this analogy, this linkage between the body and a vase, a Chinese vase in particular, one of those beautiful Chinese vases you see in museums? And then, it just kind of imagines a scene around the rain.

The thing that I think works in the poem, and that I like in the poem, or that I tried for in the poem, is that the way its associations have to do not with the body but with the mind—because the mind is what keeps free associating. The mind keeps moving off, and the mind keeps leaving the body to go off into these very, very dreamy states—you start imagining snowing in the mountains, and the Urals, and the wastes of Russia that have edged into China. I mean that's going very far from your first idea of a poem about your body. The idea is: How far can you go and then come back? That's where the poem tries to make that circle where it goes to the mountains, to the sunlit cave, to the monk's cell, to the pond. Sometimes I think that I come back to my body, and the poem then returns from these flights of fancy from this imaginative space to try and get back to something concrete, to get back to something physical, something pure, something clean—back to the body itself—which I am saying is a site of holiness.

MELISSA: There's a lyrical ending that I think is earned by the images.

ED: Well, you are trying. I mean, I hope so. Yes, you are trying to get back to that lyrical image, to that lyrical moment where you get something pure, because, again, the idea here is to forget the impossible weight of being human. The weight is tre-

> *You come like a penitent, a pilgrim, or a poet, or a whore, or a murderer or the opposite—a very young girl. You either come as an innocent, or you come in as someone really experienced—someone complicit—to someplace holy, but that holy place is your own body.*

mendous, and you're trying to fix something that is inside. You come like a penitent, a pilgrim, or a poet, or a whore, or a murderer or the opposite—a very young girl. You either come as an innocent, or you come in as someone really experienced—someone complicit—to someplace holy, but that holy place is your own body.

MELISSA: Would you read "Wild Gratitude"?

ED: Sure. In this poem, my cat Zooey gets literary immortality and fame by her association with a great cat out of literature, and that's Christopher Smart's cat, Jeoffry. And I'll just say that in the 18th century, Christopher Smart wrote a really wonderful poem called "Jubilate Agno" from a mental hospital, and there are three quotes in this poem from Christopher Smart's poem. He praises the postmaster general and all conveyancers of letters, he calls his cat Jeoffry, the "servant of a living God duly and daily serving Him," and he calls the mouse "a creature of great personal valor," which I have always liked.

Wild Gratitude

Tonight when I knelt down next to our cat, Zooey,
And put my fingers into her clean cat's mouth,
And rubbed her swollen belly that will never know kittens,
And watched her wriggle onto her side, pawing the air,
And listened to her solemn little squeals of delight,
I was thinking about the poet, Christopher Smart,
Who wanted to kneel down and pray without ceasing
In everyone of the splintered London streets,

And was locked away in the madhouse at St. Luke's
With his sad religious mania, and his wild gratitude,
And his grave prayers for the other lunatics,
And his great love for his speckled cat, Jeoffry.
All day today—August 13, 1983—I remembered how
Christopher Smart blessed this same day in August, 1759,
For its calm bravery and ordinary good conscience.

This was the day that he blessed the Postmaster General
"And all conveyancers of letters" for their warm humanity,
And the gardeners for their private benevolence
And intricate knowledge of the language of flowers,
And the milkmen for their universal human kindness.
This morning I understood that he loved to hear—
As I have heard—the soft clink of milk bottles
On the rickety stairs in the early morning,

And how terrible it must have seemed
When even this small pleasure was denied him.
But it wasn't until tonight when I knelt down
And slipped my hand into Zooey's waggling mouth
That I remembered how he'd called Jeoffry "the servant
Of the Living God duly and daily serving Him,"
And for the first time understood what it meant.

Because it wasn't until I saw my own cat
Whine and roll over on her fluffy back
That I realized how gratefully he had watched
Jeoffry fetch and carry his wooden cork
Across the grass in the wet garden, patiently
Jumping over a high stick, calmly sharpening

His claws on the woodpile, rubbing his nose
Against the nose of another cat, stretching, or
Slowly stalking his traditional enemy, the mouse,
A rodent, "a creature of great personal valour,"
And then dallying so much that his enemy escaped.

And only then did I understand
It is Jeoffry—and every creature like him—
Who can teach us how to praise—purring
In their own language,
Wreathing themselves in the living fire.

MELISSA: Wow! That was great too. So, we were talking earlier about how poems come from different places, and I'm assuming you loved the Christopher Smart poem and probably had that on your mind for a while as you watched your own cat.

ED: I had the Christopher Smart poem on my mind for a couple years before I ever wrote the poem "Wild Gratitude." This is the title poem of my second book, *Wild Gratitude.* The last phrase, as you know, became the title of my new and selected poems *The Living Fire.* In my first book, *For the Sleepwalkers*, I wrote a poem about Christopher Smart in which he is the speaker, and I imagined him in a kind of wild, crazed meditation in the mental asylum in London in the 18th century.

So, Christopher Smart has been with me for a long time as a poet. But it occurred to me one day when I was in Houston, many years after I had been reading Smart, when I was playing with my cat, that it would be amusing to try to see what would happen if I paralleled my playing with my cat and Christopher Smart playing with his cat, Jeoffry. It seemed to me to be so comical that I wanted to see what would happen, so I began to structure the poem as a series of parallels (I do this, he does that), and then I decided that I would set the poem on the very same day as his poem, creating an anniversary and then seeing what it would yield. So, the poem is the working through of this comparison to see what you will get, and, basically, it's a kind of education.

What does Christopher Smart teach you? Is it to go back and forth between your own cat and Christopher Smart's cat? And then, what does the cat teach you? So, the poem becomes structured. I recently read a book called *Poetry in Person: 25 Years of Conversation with America's Poets*. It's based on class discussions and interviews with poets with a wonderful teacher named Pearl London. I went to Pearl London's class, and I had given her manuscripts of the poem, and I recently saw these in the transcript of the interview which I had done in the late '80s, and I discovered that the poem for the longest time was called "August 13." So, you tell me, which is the better title, "August 13" or "Wild Gratitude"?

MELISSA: It doesn't have the same ring, does it?

ED: It does not. But, you could see why I called it that—because that's the date of the poem, and that's where it started. Then at a certain point in the writing of the poem, very far along, I discovered this phrase leaping out at me, which I thought had a lot of power and which I discovered in the writing of it, the phrase "wild gratitude."

MELISSA: I was thinking about that title, *Wild Gratitude,* actually, in the context of your idea about how poetry defamiliarizes words and then brings them back to the reader again, and I think I'm really seeing that in the poems you read—and particularly in "Wild Gratitude"—even in the title itself. The poem makes me think of the words "wild" and "gratitude" in totally new ways. Can you talk a bit about that in your own poem and as a technique in poetry?

ED: Well, this is something that poetry does when it works. I mean you have one idea of the word "wild" you have one idea of "gratitude" and when you put them together, something happens. And, you know, I like that phrase "wild gratitude," which is why I hit upon it first in the poem, then in the title, then in the title of my book—because it seemed to stand for something beyond the very phrase itself. I like it because it's got a feeling of something that's extravagant, something that's not exactly in control. I mean, what is wild gratitude? It's gratitude beyond just your relief or your thankfulness. It is some kind of uncontrollable gratitude.

The thing we've been talking about with the creative process—your gratitude, your feeling of blessing—is something that is not entirely rational. And, so, I like the feeling of extravagance in that. I think poetry can put you in the space of the feeling. It's a feeling I think we have all had. I think we all have had moments when we feel so blessed by something, so overwhelmed, that we feel that our gratitude is even incommensurate, so we feel we have a wild gratitude, not a regular gratitude.

MELISSA: Although I would have never thought to say it that way...

ED: That's the idea. That's why you are trying to write poetry. That's what you hope will happen. I mean the thing about poetry, unlike, let's say, reading the newspaper is that when you read the newspaper, you remember the story, but you forget the way in which the thing was said. The story is what's important. We all remember it, but you threw out the newspaper because the way in which it was said doesn't matter. In fact, the newspaper tries to make that as clear as possible—that the way it's written isn't supposed to matter. What's being written is all that counts. In poetry, the way in which it's being said is inseparable from what's being said. You can't throw away the poem and just remember the story when you read "Wild Gratitude." You can't go around and say, "well, there's this poem about a guy who plays with his cat, and he remembers Christopher Smart playing with his cat." That's not the poem. The way in which the poem is written is saying the thing is inseparable from what's being said. I mean, that's why Ezra Pound said, "poetry is news that stays news."

MELISSA: It's so true. Even when you mentioned the other Christopher Smart poem from your first book, the thing that came into my mind was not what the poem was about, but these lines I remembered—the final line, especially: "it's always snowing in the country of the mad."

ED: Yes, that's it.

MELISSA: It's such a powerful line.

ED: This is what you're seeking in poetry. You can't control it, but you are seeking something that will be memorable—some putting together of words in a way that, for some magical reason, you can't get out of your head, like a tune—something that stays inside you, and you don't know exactly why.

You know, sometimes you read poems, and the poem, mostly, you forget, and then something stays with you. Some formulation means something to you, and it sticks. And when it sticks with a lot of people, you have something that lasts.

I didn't set out with the idea of wild gratitude in writing my poem about Christopher Smart. I set out with the idea that I had already loved Christopher Smart, and I was moved by his going through the London streets and asking people to pray with him and his story about being locked away in the

This is what you're seeking in poetry. You can't control it, but you are seeking something that will be memorable—some putting together of words in a way that, for some magical reason, you can't get out of your head, like a tune—something that stays inside you, and you don't know exactly why.

mad house, St. Luke's, and I loved his poem "Jubilate Agno." But the poem began really with a playful idea about: let's see what would happen if we went back and forth between me playing with my cat in 1983 and Christopher Smart playing with his cat in 1759.

What I came to was that the ordinary life that we take so for granted has tremendous power for someone who has had it taken away from him. Christopher Smart is so crazed for the ordinary things—the postmaster general and the milkman and the cat—because they have been denied him. From this realm of the mad, these things take on a kind of magical power. And, so, I wanted to go back and take that sense of the blessedness of the ordinary and make that my poem. Because that is what I learned in that poem. After all, its not just Jeoffry; it's every creature like him who teaches us how to praise.

MELISSA: I've noticed that you are getting more direct in your poetry as time passes.

ED: Yes, that's true.

MELISSA: And there's more space around the lines, more vulnerability—an increased generosity and fearlessness. I'm just wondering how you see your own evolution as a poet. Are these changes intentional or are they just happening over time?

ED: I would say that they both happen over time, and they are intentional. It's hard for me to separate all of this out, but it's certainly true that as I've gotten older, and as I have sort of earned my credentials, I have been less interested in the flashing of the cards and the flashing all the things I can do formally.

I'm sort of getting down to my own human truth. Over the years, I have come to value directness in poetry, as I value it in people—more and more. So, I tried to pare down some of the extravagances of my poetic youth to try to get at some emotional core which has been important to me as I have gotten older. So, that's been a process.

MELISSA: And, do you also notice that you prefer to now read poetry that's more direct? Have your reading preferences changed with your writing intention?

ED: I can't say that my reading has changed. I think that maybe I find certain things more satisfying now and other things less satisfying. But I have always read widely, and I continue to read widely, and I don't feel that I'm reading particularly for verification of my own ideas or my own methods. So, I continue to read all different kinds of things and all different kinds of poetry. It's true that things that are more direct, and things that have a kind of high emotional quotient, often speak more powerfully to me than other kinds of things.

MELISSA: I was actually thinking about how you often tell young readers and writers that in order to be great writers of poetry they also need to be great readers of poetry.

ED: Young poets don't like to hear this. They don't like to hear it when I say there's never been a great poet in the history of poetry who also hasn't been a great reader of poetry. So, I do tell them, "You may be the first. I'm not saying it's not possible. You may be breaking the mold, but until now, in the long history of poetry, there has never been one who hasn't been a reader of poetry." So, this tells us something.

Poetry is made out of the human condition, but it's also made out of other poetry. And this is just the hard truth. And in order to write poetry, you need to read poetry. I know it seems so obvious, but it's apparently not. I think it's because poetry is so emotional for many people and because it's so personal, many people think they can write poetry without reading it. And of course you can, but I don't think you can write good poetry or poetry that will last without entering into the art. You can't be a great basketball player without seeing a basketball game.

MELISSA: Speaking of reading and influence, I have to say I was kind of surprised when I first found out that you had written your doctoral dissertation on Yeats, and I was wondering what kind of effect it would have on someone to study him in that kind of depth. That's such an early point in your career. Why did you choose him, and how do you feel it has impacted you as a writer?

ED: I've always loved Yeats's poetry, and I continue to love it. Although, I have to say, as I have gotten older—this won't surprise you—I've gotten less and less interested in the esoteric part of Yeats and more and more interested in the mid-dle and late work which is so direct, beginning with *Responsibilities and Other Poems* in 1904. In an introduction to *The Oxford Book of Modern Verse*, he says "everyone got down off his stilts." Now, when I was young, I was very interested in those stilts, and I was very inter-ested in Yeats's elaborate systematizing, and the esoteric doc-trine that he had. But, as I have gotten older, that doctrine is still there, and I think it's very useful in understanding the poems, but what I really admire is the great formal skill and directness of the poems. The esoteric things are still there, but it's possible to read those poems without knowing anything about them. This is one of the fantastic things about Yeats. You can read some of those late poems and not know anything about the mystical systems. The more you now about the mystical systems, the more they enhance the poems. But, they are not necessary to the poems in terms of

> *I have tried to be as ruthlessly truthful as possible about my own spiritual quest and my own spiritual longings—which are great—and my own feeling for the divine, which is great. But I can't say that I rest in it or that I have confirmed it or that I ultimately believe it. I always long for it, and that's what my poetry tries to chart.*

their direct appeal. I didn't know that when I was young, but I feel that strongly now.

MELISSA: One of the predominant themes in your poems in general is the difficulty that you've had with faith, and you have been so generous and so honest with the reader about that difficulty. I read that you described your book *Earthly Measures* as "God-hungry," and I also remember from one of your poems the haunting image of the God-shaped hole in your chest, and yet the poems that you just read, and in so many poems that I read of yours I see this profound spirituality. Would you talk about the struggle with faith and spirituality and its relationship to your writing?

ED: I feel that I have never been gifted with belief, and I think that it *is* a gift, and I don't have it. But I have always admired it, and I have always quested for something. So, I see myself as a seeker. But I'm aware that in my own work, in my own quest, there won't be any rest, and there won't be much certainty, but I seem to have a deep need to try and find something, to seek something beyond the daily, beyond the quotidian, something beyond the human. But I haven't been able to find it.

Yet, I keep longing for it, and a lot of my poetry has been to find figures who help me or enable me in this quest. A lot of poetry does this work for me of seeking, and I have tried to be honest in my poems. I have tried to be as ruthlessly truthful as possible about my own spiritual quest and my own spiritual longings—which are great— and my own feeling for the divine, which is great. But I can't say that I rest in it or that I have confirmed it or that I ultimately believe it. I always long for it, and that's what my poetry tries to chart.

My poem "A Partial History of My Stupidity" ends with a line that I have always been amused by: "I did not believe in God, who eluded me." Now, the phrase "eluded me" suggests that there is a God who is hiding from you, but you are asserting at the same time that you don't believe in him. So, it always seemed funny to me that I have a sense that there is a God who is eluding me.

In another poem, "Green Couch," I say "I am angry at God for no longer existing." That's amusing to me, because, of course, if there really wasn't any God, how could you possibly be angry at him? You are asserting that he doesn't exist, but you are also mad at him.

So, I keep finding comical ways to express this conundrum of something which is the seeking of something that you are sure must be there but for which you have skepticism that it actually exists. So, this seems to be the state that I continuously find myself in within the poetry, especially in the book *Earthly Measures*.

MELISSA: This reminds me of one of Yeats's theories that you wrote about—the idea that the best poetry really comes out of those who struggle with themselves.

ED: Yes, what he says is "we make out of the quarrel with others, rhetoric, but of the quarrel with ourselves, poetry." So, even though there's the rhetorical dimension to poetry, I have always liked that idea of the self-quarrel. I like that notion of self-conviction. I mean, the aesthetic is basically *convict thyself*. And I have always liked the way that certain poets turn the knife against themselves and I have often tried to do it myself in terms of ruthless self-scrutiny.

MELISSA: How you would say the writing itself has impacted this struggle with spirituality. I mean, we see how it is present in the writing, but how has the process of writing impacted it? Does that make sense?

ED: You mean, for my own life?

MELISSA: Yes.

ED: I don't know what to say. The writing is the practice. It's acted out. I mean, what you see is what you get. I'm not holding any secrets. I'm not really going to church every Sunday and just not telling you about it.

MELISSA: That's what I suspected.

ED: I mean it is what it is. It's just my practice.

MELISSA: I think what I'm trying to say, and what I wasn't really getting out, is that it seems to me like— and it's probably totally presumptuous of me to say this—but it seems to me, that writing *is* your spiritual practice. And what I see is that I have never known, or met, or read of anyone else who is more dedicated to poetry than you are. So I feel that you have this incredible faith in poetry that never seems to waver.

ED: That is true. I mean, if I had to say what my religion was, I would have to say that I'm afraid that has been my religion. My vocation is poetry, and my lifelong commitment has been to poetry. And I decided when I was a teenager that I wanted to be a poet. I decided when I was in college that this was my vocation, and this is what I would do, and I'm sixty years old now, and it just hasn't wavered.

MELISSA: You never feel disillusioned with poetry?

ED: Exactly. I mean, I get tired of some poets, and, believe me, I get annoyed by certain people, and I get annoyed by certain reputations. So I would say, individual poets sometimes let me down as people and sometimes their work lets me down, but *poetry itself*, the practice of poetry, and the larger church of poetry—it's a big country, and there are lots of people in it. And that practice, and that worldwide activity, has been very sustaining to me, and I, for some reason, recognize myself in it. I wanted to be part of this community of poets, living and dead—that was my dearest wish, and it just hasn't wavered. I'm not exactly sure why I felt called to this, but I was, and I'm hoping to take it all the way to the end. I feel very strongly that I sought out my alternative family in the family of poets.

MELISSA: That's a great answer. We're about to run out of time, so I'm just going to ask you a quick question. You know, I laughed when I saw an interview where you discussed *The Living Fire* and said that compiling that collection was more traumatic than you expected it to be. Could you talk about why it was traumatic and how you overcame the trauma to make the collection?

ED: I put together a *Selected Poems*. No one put a gun to my head and said I had to do it, and, so, I did it, and I thought I would enjoy it. The reason it was traumatic was that I worked very hard for my whole writing life to make individual books. Robert Frost said, "If there are 29 poems in a book, then the book itself is the 30th poem." You are looking for something in a book where it's larger than the sum of its parts. So, every book has its own journey, its own instruments, its own unities, and what I discovered when putting together *Selected Poems*—which I should have known in advance, but I hadn't thought of—was that when you are selecting certain poems and taking them out of their original books, you are losing that structure. They are no longer in relationship to each other; they are in relationship to your larger work.

It's also true how you are shoving some of the children out anyway, you are sending them to the second level, and you suddenly realize, I always cared about these poems—I worked so hard on them, and now I'm putting them in the bleachers. So, there's that. You have to select. That's the point. But then the poems lose their resonance to the collection that they were in, and that's why it was traumatic. The compensation is that I decided I was making a new book and creating a new through-line and that I would let *The Living Fire* have its own life, its own structure. I would lose certain things by taking out a lot of the poems and putting other poems in, but I had also gained something by creating a through-line that would try to represent the diversity of my work while also creating a kind of feeling, a kind of integrity, of something that was driving it.

MELISSA: That makes a lot of sense. And thank you so much for the interview, Ed. I really appreciate it.

ED: Thank you so much for the close reading, Melissa, and the deep interview. I really appreciate it. It means a lot to me.

JEFFREY DAVIS

NOVEMBER 15, 2010

MELISSA: Our interview tonight is with Jeffrey Davis, writing coach, Tiferet fiction editor, creativity consultant, and teacher. Davis is the author of the Psychology Today blog, Tracking Wonder and the books, T*he Journey from the Center to the Page: Yoga Philosophies and Practices as Muse for Authentic Writing* and City Reservoir: A Collection of Poems. Davis has stated, "Writing that reverberates with others' deep imagination strikes me as authentic. It's authentic because it comes from a source beyond the ego mind's spinning wheels. Much authentic writing then is sensuous and sensual. Verbs lick us. Images ignite our imaginations. Suggestive diction caresses us."

Can you start us off by talking about why yoga is beneficial to writing and other creative endeavors?

JEFFREY: That's certainly been the question I've been living in for a little over ten years. The short answer is that intentional self-aware yoga practice or, what I now call "Yoga as muse," does at least two or three seminal things for writers and artists and others in creative endeavors.

One is that it does instill a greater awareness of the mind and the imagination, emotions, and habits. It calms the sympathetic nervous system, and when it calms the sympathetic nervous system it calms down that hyper-rational, over-functioning facet of the mind that's always spinning. That mind is not just the doubts and fears we have—that mind's also the mind that's analyzing. It's figuring out. It's critiquing. It's the very useful part of the mind that we use to survive and function during much of the day. But there's so much more to the mind, and what happens with yoga, when that sympathetic nervous system calms down and that portion of the brain, which has been identified as largely in the cortex, quiets, then there's another part of the mind that awakens. It's that part that we often describe as intuitive, imaginative, emotional, and yoga.

What's really unique about yoga, and some traditions of Buddhism, is that these traditions give us creative people a set of handy tools to moderate our physical mind and to navigate what are going to be the inevitable challenges of crafting a creative life and changing some of our unproductive habits. So, if you become adept enough with the yoga practice, you can learn how to instill a more intuitive, dreamy state of mind. I'll give you an example of a writer I work with regularly. She's a prominent fiction writer who teaches at a high profile college, and, as with a lot of professor-writers, the job's demands and the nature of the analytical work of shopping manuscripts kind of takes a toll on the creative mind. It takes up a lot of space in the mind, and I've offered to her a sketch of a short flow of postures and harnessed breathing that I know will help her cultivate an intuitive, imaginative space probably within about 7 or so minutes of practice.

We have the mind-sets we do; we have the external circumstances in which we each live, which are constantly changing and surprising us, but yoga gives us a series of tools to talk to the mind, to alter states of awareness, whether we are going to be analytical or imaginative or intuitive. Are we going to be focused and concentrating? All of the things we desire as writers—we often just sort of wait for them to happen. "Well, I'll just wait until I feel inspired to write." I don't know about you, but if I just waited, I wouldn't be writing fiction. You might have a piece twice a year or something. So, that's not the short answer, but maybe that's the medium answer. The good stuff first.

What's really unique about yoga, and some traditions of Buddhism, is that these traditions give us creative people a set of handy tools to moderate our physical mind and to navigate what are going to be the inevitable challenges of crafting a creative life and changing some of our unproductive habits.

MELISSA: When you were talking about your client it made me think that it would be great if you could share an example of a specific exercise and how it could enhance writing or unleash a particular aspect of writing. I bring this up because your book, *The Journey From The Center To The Page*, has such a great balance between theory and practical, specific advice.

JEFFREY: That's good. Thanks. I'm glad that was your experience because that was my intention. I'd be glad to describe one brief, but very effective tool. The thing about these tools that I want to say in advance is that some people will experience immediate shifts, rather dramatically and quickly, and then they have to work on sustaining those shifts. Other people won't notice much of a difference at first, but the reason they may not notice a difference at first is because these tools work very subtly on the mind and on what cognitive psychologists call the adaptive unconscious, which is part of the unconscious constantly making decisions rather quickly—it's influenced even by things like our autonomic nervous system, our heartbeat, and our oxygenation to the brain—all these things that we're not thinking about that are part of our body's functioning. So these tools, including the one I'm going to show you, work at the level of the autonomic nervous system (which is very subtle) to shift the patterns in which our respiration works. It shifts, as I said, the oxygenation to the brain, so you have to give these tools several days sometimes before you really begin to observe their effect. So, one tool is called alternate nostril breathing and I don't know if you actually want me to lead you through it on the air, but I can at least describe it to you. Is that what you'd like?

MELISSA: I think describing it will be sufficient; then, if I feel like I don't understand, maybe you can lead me through it.

JEFFREY: I want to take you through the hand gesture because it's a little tricky to describe without seeing it.

If you were to take your thumb and index finger and place your thumb on the right side of your nose and your index on the left side of your nose, then you would close off the right nostril with your thumb and inhale slowly only through the left nostril, letting the belly relax on the inhalation. Then you close the left nostril and exhale gently, drawing the belly in on the exhalation and slowly inhaling through the right nostril. Then you close the right nostril and open the left and exhale slowly through the left and then repeat that three times or six times or nine times.

The responses vary, yet they are very consistent both in my own practice and with artists and writers with whom I work. Most of them feel an instant state of calm alertness. They feel alert, yet relaxed. They feel relaxed, but not sleepy or drowsy. I taught this even to some teenagers at an academy, some rather skeptical teen-agers, about a year ago, and many of them instantly noticed. There was this young man who was sort of surprised at how calm his adolescent mind felt and how easily he could write afterwards. So, that's just one example.

I practice a certain sequence that I call my concentration sequence, and I practice some variation of that every morning that is grounded in the lower body. What I like is

What I like is that the quiet part of the mind is down in the legs and feet if you really understand that the mind moves throughout the whole body.

that the quiet part of the mind is down in the legs and feet if you really understand that the mind moves throughout the whole body. The lower body is the quiet part of the mind. I go through a sequence. It probably only takes about 8-10 minutes every morning. That helps me focus. Twelve years ago, I could barely read the words of some of the books of literature I was to be teaching because my mind was such a mess, so I've worked long and hard every day on instilling concentration, and I can say after a dozen years, it's worked.

MELISSA: Clearly the yoga practice has enhanced your writing practice and your writing methods. Have you noticed that it's also changed the writing itself?

JEFFREY: Has it changed the quality of writing?

MELISSA: The quality or the subject matter. Have you noticed differences in your actual writing since you began yoga?

JEFFREY: Yes. It's kind of hard, of course. These cause and effect things are really tricky, but absolutely. I noticed there was a different quality of verve, of texture, and almost manic imagination the first year. My mind became sort of a metaphor machine, and I couldn't stop the metaphors.

I'm sure there's some sort of medical diagnosis for the name of what I was experiencing, but I was loving it. So, I've tempered it, but you know what's happened, Melissa, that I didn't expect, is that within the first year of practicing regularly, I did notice my concentration coming back. Really, within a matter of a couple of months. And then my imagination was on fire, but what I didn't know would happen is that my emotional armor (at the time I was a 31 year-old, overly intellectual man) just kind of broke open, and so I spent the first year crying, because I was pretty closed off emotionally.

So what does this mean for a writer? Does this mean I was just writing a bunch of emotional dreck on the page? No. At least not publicly. What it's meant is that I need to feel emotionally connected to what I'm writing. I can tell when my language is flat or when my writing spirit, whatever you want to call it, is flat, and I know ways I have to go move my body to start feeling again.

I mean, after all, feeling literally is a tactile sense, and emotions, for me, are of course, very physical. If I'm writing a short story about, say, Walter Osterhoudt, and that short story "Nail on the Head," is about a widowed carpenter, I may know next to nothing about carpentry, and I don't know anything first hand about real grief. Yet I had to find ways to really feel that grief and loss. I've experienced loss in different ways, so I tapped into deep feelings of real loss and grief to the point as I was writing I was feeling knots in my throat. I don't think I had that emotional range before my yoga practice. I think it was still an overly intellectual sort of experimental in my writing before then.

MELISSA: Yeah, you know, actually I see that from your two collections of poems. The first collection was wonderful, but I can see how it was more intellectual. The second collection, the manuscript, has a combination of intellectuality and the emotion you're talking about that comes through now.

JEFFREY: I'm glad you saw that.

MELISSA: I didn't know what it was until I heard what you just said. One last thing about the technical aspects of the practice—can you talk about the four preparations, and especially the core question, "What am I writing?"

JEFFREY: Well, the four preparations which are really outlining the first four chapters of the book— those came from reflecting upon my own obstacles. And then, as I started to share with other writers at the workshops I was teaching, I discovered, low and behold, most writers and artists share the same categories of obstacles.

These four preparations respond to those big four categories of obstacles which might be defined as: one, lack of motivation and purpose; two, a lack of time; three, lack of persistence and perseverance; and four, lack of concentration.

These four preparations respond to those big four categories of obstacles which might be defined as: one, lack of motivation and purpose; two, a lack of time; three, lack of persistence and perseverance; and four, lack of concentration. So, the four preparations respond to each of those obstacles. One is to put on the robe and write with intention. Two is to show up and shape time. Three is to stoke the creative or the writer's fire. And four is to ride the wave of concentration.

So, the first one is to put on the robe and write with intention. Putting on the robe is an image that was taught to me when I was a resident at the Zen Mountain Monastery in upstate New York when one morning during dharma talk, a monk raised the question, "Of all the things you could do with your morning, why put on the robe?"

Why put on the robe and sit and just breathe? So, it's a very similar question we writers remind ourselves: "With all the things that you could do with your life and with your day, with your morning, why put on the robe and write?"

I inverted the question. I switched the question away from "Why am I writing?" to "What am I writing for?" The question "Why am I writing?" can put you on the defensive, like, "Why aren't you out making furniture?" or "Why aren't you out making money somewhere, or, you know, feeding the poor, something like that?" So, it's not, "Why am I writing?" but "What am I writing for?"

That question just came to me one morning when I was exploring these connections and trying to feel my own sense of purpose in trying to remember how I got in this endeavor in the first place, and for me, now at this point in my life, "What is this writing for?" So I center myself with a few harnessed breathing exercises every morning. I connect with a certain part of my body, which is usually my belly and my chest space, and I ask that question, "What am I writing for?"

These are ways to get me out of my intellectual, analytical mind. These are intuitive ways to open up another part of my writer's mind, so the response might be just a physical sensation of how I want to be in this body and in this world as a writer or it might be an image or a word or a phrase.

Regardless, it always puts me in touch with something that matters as a writer. It doesn't have to be big and lofty, it just matters to me, and this is one of the first things that I guide writers and artists in to practicing. It's a beautiful way to frame your writing practice too. You know, if you were to do nothing else except sit at your desk or wherever it is you write and just breathe in and out three times and then just listen with your deepest ear to that question "What am I writing for?" you might experience a little shift. You may not get any answer and that's okay. You just live in that question for a few weeks, "What am I writing for?" and see what happens.

MELISSA: One of the compelling things to me is that you recommend asking the question every day, every time you write so that it becomes a practice that is part of the writing itself. I think it's easy to lose sight of your purpose, and that question brings you back.

JEFFREY: You're right. It does bring you back to what matters, and the practice is essential as writers. Maybe it's not every day for you, but it's our idea, those little subtle images, the little voices, the little stories—they need watering regularly; they need to be paid attention to regularly.

MELISSA: Jeffrey, because you are the *Tiferet* fiction editor, I'm sure many of the listeners would like to know what you look for when selecting manuscripts for the journal. Will you tell us a little bit about that process and your specific criteria?

JEFFREY: As an editor and coach for a variety of writers around the country, I'm often in this role of thinking about readers ultimately and what their experience is going to be. So, specifically, I'd say, one of the first qualities I listen for is just some confident authority.

There's something in the command of syntax and story that can signal to me from the first sentence that I and my readers would be in good hands with this story-teller or this narrator. I can usually hear it in the first few sentences.

The second is a distinct voice, especially if the story is written in first person. I want to hear a voice that's a little larger than life or that has a unique slant on the world or an experience, you know, something that I'm not likely to encounter in every day life. It's fiction after all, so I want that voice to stand out if it's written in first person. It shouldn't be contrived, but I want it to be distinct, and if it's written in third person, then I still want the narrator's voice to be distinct in some ways.

> *"It's easy to practice Zen in the monastery amongst your fellow monks, with your scriptures, and bells, and drums, but it's another thing to practice in town, at night, among the people, in the bars and brothels."*

The third quality, which is probably related, has to do with character. I think most readers of fiction relish reading fiction because they are drawn into a unique, subjective point of view, or imagined experience, and I have to tell you, that my taste in characters is with the sort of un-noble and imperfect and the flawed and the vain and the presumptuous and the prejudiced. So, I'm interested in those flawed characters in some ways, not to say that every story I would accept needs to have a flawed character, but those are the ones that I'm interested in.

That reminds me of a brief story from Zen. Could I tell that in relation to this?

MELISSA: Please do.

JEFFREY: It's relevant to our discussion, particularly with *Tiferet*. When I was a student at the Zen Monastery, I was flipping through some books in their library and I came across this story I have never forgotten, where a Zen monk apparently cracked out of the monastery almost every night one week and would hang out in the bars and the brothels. Finally his fellow monks found out, and they said, "What are you doing in the bars and brothels? You are disgracing us. You are not a good monk." And he said, "It's easy to practice Zen in the monastery amongst your fellow monks, with your scriptures, and bells, and drums, but it's another thing to practice in town, at night, among the people, in the bars and brothels."

I say this specifically to the listeners who are thinking of submitting to *Tiferet* because people often think that because we are a journal of spiritual literature that we're not looking for real literature that engages the world. So, again, I'm very interested in characters who are flawed, the underdogs, the spiritually unfit, who might have one redeeming moment in the span of a short story.

So, the fourth quality has to do with, maybe, what I'd say, is story and consequence. Something needs to happen and in a short story things need to be happening on almost every page, so I'm less interested in meditations disguised as short stories or in long interior monologues that are couched as short stories. If you think about consequence exponentially and spiritually, karma and spirituality have to do with making decisions.

So, as the fiction editor, I'm curious about questions in stories like, what happens when we make a bad decision, what happens when in spite of our good intention we still screw up, or what happens when we make a good decision that goes wrong? Those are questions about the human experience that I think the best fiction can play out and explore, and that's all about karma in our lives. So, I'd just say, if there are writers who are listening who say, "Oh, gosh, I've always had difficulty with story and plot," then put your character in a precarious situation with another character who wants something very different from your main character, and have your character make bad decisions, and see what happens and imagine the possibilities, and let your character get into trouble.

So, story and consequence. Is that good? Is this enough? I've got more.

MELISSA: Please go on. This is fabulous, way better than I expected.

JEFFREY: There's something else which is related—it has to do with movement. I learned a practice from another editor years ago who learned this practice from Ezra Pound, no less. When Pound would edit short stories, supposedly he'd read the first paragraph of the short story, and if the language, craft and story merited reading more, he'd leap to the last paragraph, and if there was some connection between the first paragraph and the last paragraph, some progression, however minute, then he'd bother to read the middle.

So, I've been known to read this way too, but with *Tiferet*, with the stories that are sent to me, I usually do go ahead and read from beginning to end, but then I go back and re-read. If this has really taken me in, then I go back, and I look somewhat at structure and movement. I look at the beginning, middle, and end. The exceptional stories have some sense of architecture, and I think those are well worth the time of *Tiferet* readers.

Also, surprise. I'm looking for surprise. I'm a very annoying person to, say, watch an episode of Law & Order with, because I'm always trying to predict what's going to happen in every scene, and I think I read stories this way too sometimes, and I don't want to be able to predict what's going to happen.

I want to be delighted or terrified or surprised in some ways. And, for *Tiferet*, I do think, yes, that something the story needs to offer is either some small light of redemption or some indirect insight

> *...something the story needs to offer is either some small light of redemption or some indirect insight into the complex nature of being human and seeing peace in this complicated world.*

into the complex nature of being human and seeing peace in this complicated world. But, I say that very guardedly, because I'm not inviting lessons at the end of the short stories.

MELISSA: Yes, you are in need of an ending.

JEFFREY: Right.

MELISSA: Okay. That was a fabulous answer.

JEFFREY: Good.

MELISSA: You made a lot of important clarifications there. Let's let the listeners hear a little bit of your own writing. Will you read the first two pages of "Swallow Koans" and provide a brief summary of the story as well?

JEFFREY: Sure. "Swallow Koans" is a short story I wrote several years ago. It's published in the anthology, *You Are Not Here and Other Works Of Buddhist Fiction*, that Keith Kachtick edited.

So, this short story is set in Nebraska in a small town. The main character—his name is Arthur—he's an artist, and as the story opens you learn that he's been obsessed for a couple of weeks with barn swallows, and he doesn't really know why. But like writers and artists do, he follows his obsession, and you find out that his wife left him about a year before the story opens, and he tries through-out the story to continue practicing Zen meditation with little luck because his inner life is in such turmoil. But, gradually, by following his obsession with swallows, he gets gently entangled with another woman, and they do their dance, and the story alternates between scenes related to swallows and scenes related to this unfolding rela-tionship. So, "Swallow Koans":

It starts with an inscription of a print that Arthur is looking at:

Barn Swallow. Hirundo Americana. Male. 1. Female. 2. No. 35. Plate CLXXIII. Drawn from Nature by J.J. Audubon, ERS, E.L.S. Engraved, Printed, & Colored by R. Havell. 1836.

Drawn from Nature? How many birds had Audubon killed for that drawing, Arthur wondered as he stood, sketch-pad in hand, in

Nebraska's Sagataw Museum of Art. How does it feel to ensnare a bird, hold its tiny body with one hand, and with the other snap its neck? Arthur scratched the tufts of his wavy black hair.

He was obsessed, no doubt about it. Since a pair of swallows began nesting in the barn on the farm he'd rented alone for the past year, Arthur couldn't close his eyes without swallows circling his skull. The obsession was a welcomed diversion though—twelve months ago his wife had left him. Cloistered in the farmhouse, Arthur feared he'd become a topic of conversation among the gossipers at Garland's Depot. The hot-shot native son. The successful painter. The Zen Buddhist, whatever that might mean. He hoped they still thought of him as one of their own. But, since last winter, his only excursions beyond his house had been the weekly ninety-minute drive to the museum where he would stare for hours at the canvases the way he gazed as a boy at the stained glass windows of First Nebraska Baptist Church.

Arthur's worn, nimble hands tried, unsuccessfully, to capture in charcoal and corrugated paper the swallow's unsettled peace. Her nest was gray and daubed with hints of cedar brown. Straw-like lines straggled from the nest's bottom as if the bird's mud house had grown whiskers. The raggedy kind he sported the summer he met Andi. The nest reminded Arthur of the open-roofed eco-home they dreamed of building into the side of the hill where for six years they lived together. That particular dream lasted only a few months before Andi let her desires light on something else.

Andi. A woman whose high spiritual aspirations could throw any man off balance.

"Hi. I'm Andi. I'm a shaman", she announced when Arthur first met her while hiking alone on the High Plains Trail. She was on her knees, digging out burdock root with a trowel. "Burdock's great for soul retrieval rituals," she told him, a little light of breath. Arthur smiled. He hoped not patronizingly. It's not every day you find a fresh-eyed woman in eastern Nebraska calling herself a shaman and wearing a trowel holster. And she was beautiful. Twenty-eight years young, she told him, with enormous blue eyes, an unbridled spirit, and what he knew within minutes was an innocent but profound drive to be extraordinary. Forty years old then, Arthur found her irresistible. By the end of the next autumn, they were married.

When Arthur's pencil began to move again, his breathing relaxed. The swallow peeked over the nest's edge, her rust-colored head with its iridescent blue mask peering back to admire the sleek, midnight-blue strokes composing her smooth body and elegantly forked tail. She appeared at home, completely at ease. Another swallow was visible below her. His blue-black head pointing in the opposite direction. *Fool*, Arthur wanted to say. *Watch out.*

MELISSA: Thank you. That was great. Your writing is such a perfect example of what you teach, and in this story in particular, I noticed the parallelism between the Koans and the paintings, and Arthur and the birds—the technique is so subtle and organic that I really hesitate to call it something as obvious as metaphor or symbolism, but it demonstrates your point in The Journey from the Center to the Page about how authentic metaphor not used as artifice can enhance rather than cloud understanding. Can you talk about authentic versus artificial metaphor and how a writer can know when they've tapped into something authentic, as you did here.

JEFFREY: That's a great question. I think this is a really important subject, and I would say the best way for a writer of fiction to go is to really immerse himself or herself in the main charac-ter's point of view and sub-

> *...the best way for a writer of fiction to go is to really immerse himself or herself in the main character's point of view and subjective reality, and that means really trying to walk as that character,*

jective reality, and that means really trying to walk as that character, and this is in part why going back to the yoga practice helps me as a fiction writer—because, I am literally moving to feel that charac-ter's body and what life is like from that character's point of view. So, if you think about it, every short story is a little world told from a certain point of view.

All frames of reference, all frames of comparisons, will stem from that subjective point of view. So, if I were writing a short story from the point of view of an accountant, that accountant is going to make a lot of comparisons to the bottom line and to balance sheets and things of that nature, right?

But if it's an accountant living in New York City, and suddenly the narrator—let's say, it's told from third person, limited point of view—and suddenly, the narrator makes some random meta-phorical comparison to the way streams run in the woods, and those images bear no relationship to the eight pages of the short story, then that's something I would say is inorganic as a met-aphor. It doesn't fit the subjective scheme of the short story's world.

So, what happens, is when you immerse yourself in that subjective point of view, the comparisons will arise naturally. That's the comparison that's going to work here. And you will feel when it's not right. It will feel forced. It will feel like trying to stick a "Happy Birthday" sticker on a gift and just kind of slapping it on just because it's a birthday present. It's not really an organic part of the package, so to speak.

MELISSA: I totally understand what you're saying. It's the difference between a metaphor that connects to the world of the story or just a clichéd metaphor that just comes up because it's something that's in the context of general culture or whatever.

JEFFREY: Yes, general culture, and it might even be coming out of the writer's framework instead of the character's framework, instead of the imagined world's framework.

MELISSA: That's a great point. I love in the end of "Swallow Koans" when Rosemary asks Arthur if he's thought about going back to doing more self-portraits, and he responds by saying that he's beginning to think that's all he's been doing by drawing the birds. It's such a wonderful comment about how everything we do is, in essence, a self-portrait, even if the subject is seemingly different from ourselves. Can you talk about this, especially as it pertains to your own writing?

JEFFREY: Yeah, you know, I had kind of forgotten about that little part, but it's actually essential to the story, and it's essential to my view of what writing is. So, I've never—even when I was in my early twenties and taking myself a bit too seriously as a writer—I even then didn't lean toward the idea of writing as self-expression. That just didn't resonate to me. I didn't want to write to express myself. So, there are other phrases that resonate with me in my writing. Self-exploration and self-expression. From my point of view, the self is mainly involved. There's some steady self that I'm finally, after forty-five years, really, starting to connect with and understand, and then there are other elements of the self that are parts of our personality. Maybe I could use a good metaphor like a pantheon. Let's say there's a pantheon where there are multiple gods and goddesses, and they are all expressing all these different parts of human drama and human emotional drama. If you were to think of yourself as a pantheon, then you'd understand how to apply yourself instead of pretending you are just one thing.

And, so, yes, a short story is in many ways, for me, an exploration of myself or my selves. It's not always deliberately so, but it's also an expansion of the self. Maybe two short stories will really illustrate the contrast. "Swallow Koans" definitely has some closer autobiographical references than most of the short stories I write now. But, all of those characters were different kinds of explorations of myself in some ways.

Rosemary, Arthur, and Andy, were all different facets of myself, you could say. With "Nail on the Head" and some of these other short stories, I'm writing from first person

> *If you were to think of yourself as a pantheon, then you'd understand how to apply yourself instead of pretending you are just one thing.*

point of view where I, my personality, my biographical self that you know as "Jeffrey Davis" has nothing in common with a widowed carpenter or a woman who's discovered online dating and is running around trying to get as many dates as she can in eight days.

I don't have anything in common biographically with these characters, yet there are parts of my personality that I can also explore. I can explore the curmudgeonly cranky self in Walter Osterhoudt, or I can explore other facets of the self. It's not a conscious endeavor, usually with my fiction, to say, "I'm going to explore this part of myself." Rather, it's a conscious endeavor to say, "I just want to explore this character's reality and what that life is like."

I overhead a conversation in the waiting room of the family clinic where we go, and it was just myself and this woman on a cell phone, and I got to hear her half of this conversation, and at first I was annoyed, and then I realized I had something really good, and I pulled out my notebook and acted like I was making my grocery list, but I was really quoting her.

I thought, "Oh, my God. I only have this other voice that's been running around in my head," and so I thought, "Okay, what would it be like to be a woman this age, in these circumstances, who discovers online dating?" What is that reality like, and what is that world like? So I immersed myself in that.

MELISSA: And I have to say, that's a fabulous story, "Eight Men, Seven Days, Two Breasts." I know you're still finishing it. Do you know yet where you'll be publishing it so people can look for it when it comes out?

JEFFREY: No. I'll let you know. I thought I had finished it, but then I unraveled it more. I'm very excited about that short story. I'm excited about the series of short stories where I'm really assuming different first person points of view. They're all roughly based on the area where I live in upstate New York in a little farming hamlet, and there is just such a rich variety of characters there that I love. They are all so quirky and challenging to love in person, but in fiction I can love them.

MELISSA: I understand. And when you finish that story and decide to publish it, you should post a link to the publication on the Tiferet blog because people just really need to read that story. It is so funny.

JEFFREY: Thank you. I will.

MELISSA: Terrific. I want to make sure we have time to hear your poetry too. I just realized that both the story and the poem have birds as the subject matter. I didn't do that intentionally, but if you could read "Heron," that would be great.

JEFFREY: Sure. That's wonderful. I won't set it up. I'll just read it.

Heron

Weightless stone with wings here on water
Here on the brink of day as skies third eye winks behind
Orange clouds
In the wish of dawn
In the wish of water
Find a fish that calls you
And take in your beak then down your long throat

These aches of needy company

These tugs from insistent voices

Then lift me with you

Weightless limb with wings

That we may blend in among the willow

And early light the hue of blue semblance

Steady and still

Here on the limb are wings and head fold in our form along closed eyelid

The quiet confidence of being alone wades and are awake

Here in pale light

Here on water

Here on air

Heron

MELISSA: That was lovely. Thank you. The reading was wonderful. I'm not sure if people necessarily picked up on things that are visible on the page, but one of the things is the repetition of the phrase "here on," which gains momentum in the last stanza and then gradually turns into "heron." That made me think about your ideas about allowing the logic of sound to create its own meaning in the poem, and the idea of allowing oneself to follow the intuitive logic of language and syntax. Will you talk about that?

JEFFREY: Oh, God. Yeah, I could talk for an hour about that. I love trying to explain something as ethereal as

It has something to do with my sense still that there is something, I don't know, sacred, spellbinding, in following the sounds of language. I mean, what is a spell but the right combination of words to alter awareness or the right combination of letters?

following the logic of sounds. I would say, from early on, you can hear some of this in my poems in *City Reservoir*, but early on, I was also drawn as much, if not more, to sounds in language rather than semantics. It has something to do with my sense still that there is something, I don't know, sacred, spellbinding, in following the sounds of language. I mean, what is a spell but the right combination of words to alter awareness or the right combination of letters?

So, I write this way often, in both poetry, fiction, sometimes in non-fiction, but it usually gets me in trouble in non-fiction. I usually write really not knowing where I'm going when I'm drafting. I'm listening, and I'm listening where to go next, and I lay out some words, unfold from an image or an impulse or a phrase or a character's voice in fiction, and I'm listening. I'm listening to the way the sound of one word is going to suggest another.

So, this poem is a good example. I don't want to analyze my own poem. That would be obnoxious. But, there's a lot of internal rhyme and there's a lot of sound quality in this poem, and it's the sound, that almost incantatory rhythm, especially in poems, that draws me in. But, just about process, I would say, and I've done this in my workshops before, I have stopped people in the middle of what they're writing, and it will annoy them at first, but I'm trying to train their ear. I would say, "Stop and listen to the last noun that you wrote, and close your eyes, and repeat that noun over and over and over again, like a mantra, until you start hearing other words suggested by similar sounds and sound qualities. They don't have to rhyme. They just might sound similar. And weave one of those words in your next line or your next sentence." It's just a way to tune people in to the peripheries of their imagination.

MELISSA: I think also, as shown by your poem, following sound is to some extent a more fundamental way to connect to the subject, in addition to the logicality that's already happening. Okay, one last question: I know you're the author of the Psychology Today blog Tracking Wonder. Can you talk about the importance of wonder for writing and our lives, and, specifically, how we can cultivate wonder as adults?

JEFFREY: Oh, boy. We can sit for an hour on this one. I'll just say why it's so important to writers. It's where imagination begins, frankly. Wonder is that capacity to be open and to be spellbound by the smallest things. It's the sounds of words or the blue gray loom of a November sky at dusk, and it's that non-sophisticated openness. It's where stories and poems and art and design and world-changing projects often begin.

It seems as if every AWP *The Writer's Chronicle* issue that has come out recently has a writer who expresses something similar, you know, the former poet laureate Ted Kooser says basically the same thing, and Pam Houston several months ago said basically that, "All writing begins with the amazement at small things." So, wonder also puts us in a space of not knowing, and it puts us in questions more than answers, and I think it's that not knowing that leads many of us to write in the first place.

We write stories because we have questions. We write poems because we have questions. And it also opens us up to that space of stillness. It leads to deep connection, absorbing another person, which leads to compassion, and we could talk also about why compassion is necessary, but I think some of the best novelists and poets—Faulkner, Kingsolver, Ted Hughes, and several lesser knowns—can embody the voices and figures of the 10,000 things of the animals and human beings on our planet. So, how can we cultivate it as adults? Well, you could read my blog at www.psychology-today.com because it's hard for me to summarize really quickly how you can cultivate it.

MELISSA: Definitely. We should point people to that blog because almost every entry talks about that.

JEFFREY: It does. Specifically, it's addressing adults, and you know, I'm wanting to create wonder for adults. It's not just children and babies who experience wonder. We adults experience it at a whole other level. So, that's my "wonder spiel."

MELISSA: Great. We're almost out of time Do you have any upcoming events or publications you would like to announce?

JEFFREY: This is my dormant time, which means I'm on deep retreat and hermitage. I'm working on a book, and, there is a poem coming out in the next issue of "Sentence: A Journal of Prose Poetics," that Brian Clements edits and publishes. I'll be leading retreats which you can find out about at www.trackingwonder.com.

FLOYD SKLOOT

DECEMBER 9, 2010

MELISSA: Our interview tonight is with Floyd Skloot, author of seventeen books, including works of poetry, fiction, and non-fiction. Skloot is a three-time winner of the Pushcart Prize, and he has also been honored with the Pen USA Literary Award, two Pacific NW Booksellers Book Awards, an Independent Publisher's Book Award, and two Oregon Book Awards. The Harvard Review calls Skloot "a poet of singular skill and subtle intelligence," and the Washington Post calls him "a tribute to the creative spirit." *Poets & Writers Magazine* recently named him one of 50 of the Most Inspiring Writers in the World.

Hi, Floyd. Can you start by telling our listeners who aren't familiar with your life story about the virus that attacked your brain, causing the traumatic brain injury, and how that has impacted your life and your writing?

FLOYD: About 22 years ago, on December 7, 1988, I took a plane from Portland, Oregon to Washington, D.C. and the doctors are fairly certain that it was during that flight that I contracted a virus through the plane's re-circulating air. It targeted my brain for a mix of reasons. My immune system wasn't able to handle it, and the virus left me totally disabled. It took 15 years to be able to walk without a cane, and I have been struggling for all of the 22 years with the neurological damage that resulted—cognitive damage, particularly. How's that?

MELISSA: That's perfect. I know it pertains to some of your subject matter, and I wanted to make sure people understood about that up front. Also, I was thinking that one of the things writers are really great at is coming up with excuses to not write, yet here you've been presented with one of the greatest excuses to not write, and you have just pushed forward and kept writing. Do you have advice for how other writers can persevere when facing obstacles? It doesn't necessarily have to be a health obstacle.

FLOYD: I always feel awkward trying to give anybody advice, particularly writing advice. But what I would say is that, in my case, writing felt so essential. I was a writer before I got sick, and it seemed to be an illness that was meant to silence me, so I had a very powerful feeling that I needed to find a way to reclaim my voice from what was happening to me—to reclaim my voice from what I always thought of as the holes I had fallen into—the lesions in my brain. I needed to find a way back.

So, for me, writing was an integral part of how I was going to live my life: as a writer being able to describe what had happened to me—what it felt like, and what I did, and how I began putting myself back together. I don't think I could have done that without the writing.

So, the writing wasn't just the way to describe it, but it was the thing that enabled me to begin working with the fragments of memory and thought that were left and to discover how they fit together and where they were leading me.

> *A pressure built up. It was clear to me that there was something enormous broken inside of me because I wasn't able to do what I needed to do as a writer—I wasn't able to make sense of what my life was and what I was feeling and what I was remembering. The thing that was missing was writing about it.*

MELISSA: That really, really makes sense. Didn't you say in "Numbers," that there actually was a period when you weren't writing that much? I think you were involved in a career that wasn't conducive to writing. You said there was a point, long before you contracted the illness, when you realized that you were a writer, so you transitioned from being someone who wants to write to someone who "lusts to write." It was a point of no return. What do you think led you to that point?

FLOYD: Back all those years—almost, I guess, 40 years now—I was silent after writing for a few years at the very beginning of my writing life in my very early 20s. I took this job in the world outside of the world of writing and was silent for a little over a year or maybe two years, if I remember right.

A pressure built up. It was clear to me that there was something enormous broken inside of me because I wasn't able to do what I needed to do as a writer—I wasn't able to make sense of what my life was and what I was feeling and what I was remembering. The thing that was missing was writing about it. Pressure had built up to where I realized I needed to find a way to make time despite having a full-time job, despite raising a child, and despite becoming a very serious competitive long-distance runner.

I needed to also find room to write. I was not going to cohere if I didn't do that. I hope that answers your question.

MELISSA: Oh, it absolutely does, and I can see how that correlates to a lot of your writing as well. I'm thinking of the little boy in the essay "The Wink of the Zenith." I was so touched by his blending of fantasy and reality and how you could see that this child who wasn't yet writing was already a writer. Do you know what I mean?

FLOYD: I do know what you mean, and it's something I came to understand in writing about that period of my life. It was a "Wow: I was already doing that" feeling. The only piece that was missing was the words on the page. But I was already imagining how my world cohered.

MELISSA: So, in a sense, putting words on paper was just bringing to the surface what you already were.

FLOYD: Yes. It's true. It was just who I was and who I needed to be, and I needed to get out of my own way.

MELISSA: I've noticed that you just have this incredible ability to move from genre to genre, and, to me, it seems that you are equally at home in each genre. Do you have a preferred genre or one in which you feel more comfortable in than the others?

FLOYD: I was a poet first, and I believe that I am still a poet first. Everything springs from the poetry.

MELISSA: Good. I was right.

FLOYD: From the very way that thoughts and feelings begin to get shaped in rhymes and images, to the whole feeling—the whole sense of the need to be as compressed and accurate as possible in every word, every phrase, every sentence, every line—I think it all emerges from poetry and from the discipline of writing. A lot of times, when I'm dealing with material in a poem, it will become clear to me that I need to go further. I need more room than a poem—or the kind of poems I write allows me, so something that I have written about in a poem will begin to appear in an essay or even fiction. I plagiarize myself quite literally.

MELISSA: I think that's wonderful.

FLOYD: I feel that the work is all of a piece. I recognize that, of course, there's a difference between writing poetry and writing essays and writing memoirs and writing fiction, but, to me, it's all a complete body of work. And it all holds together for me.

MELISSA: I agree. Do you ever go in the other direction—start larger, like with an essay, or a novel, and then take the same subject matter and bring it into a poem?

FLOYD: That has occasionally happened, and it most often happened when a fragment or a bit that I had been working with in a longer prose piece no longer fit there and declared itself as something slightly different, as separate. Then I realized it was something that I need to handle in the genre of poetry.

MELISSA: There's an amazing description of Toomey's in your prose, and then also there's the poem "Toomey's Diner." They are not the same, but they are both beautiful, elaborate descriptions. As a reader, you can't tell which one came first.

FLOYD: Also, Toomey's Diner appears in a scene in my novel, *The Open Door*.

So, it began with a poem. I was visiting my brother in California during the last year of his life. He was slowly dying from the complications of diabetes—kidney failure. He was on dialysis. Beverly, my wife, and I would fly down to northern California, and initially it was maybe once every two or three months—then it became once every month, and then once every couple of weeks, as his time grew shorter.

We would spend time sitting together in his living room, and, you know, you had this brain damaged man—me—with fractured and scattered memories, and you had my brother, who, as dialysis wore on, was also experiencing neurological complications from the toxic build up, and we were pretty memory-damaged, the both of us. We would sit there and be silent a lot, and then every once in a while a memory would surface, and we would mention it. As I was sitting with him, I remember saying to him, "You know, Phil, I remember we used to get up Sunday mornings with Dad, and before we would go to Coney Island or Prospect Park or wherever we were going, we would go out to a diner somewhere. Am I right?"

He nodded and said, "Toomey's Diner." And, as soon as he said "Toomey's Diner," the whole environment just opened up for me, and I was there in a flash. When I got home from that visit I wrote the poem, "Toomey's Diner." If I remember right, it appeared in *The Hudson Review* and then was posted on *Poetry Daily,* where Toomey's daughter found it. She got in touch with me, and then Toomey's other daughter, and Toomey's son—they all got in touch, and they said, "You remembered it just as it was. It was all true." They told me they'd sold the diner.

Hearing their voices and their enthusiasm, I realized there was more there for me. I need to explore not just Toomey's Diner, but also the Sunday morning world with my family, and that led to an essay. So, one thing led to another and unfolded. I'm not sure I'm done. In fact, I know I'm not done yet with the Toomey's, because I got a phone call earlier this year that one of the Toomey children was about to turn 70, and the gift that she wanted the most was to have me read "Toomey's Diner" to them as part of the birthday celebration.

So, how about that? You know, I have come to realize that my memories and my past are not mine alone. They are floating memories that are out there, and people are finding me and checking in and filling in holes—people I lost touch with 50 years ago. My past is very much alive in the voices of all these people who shared a little piece of it and are able to get in touch and give it back to me.

MELISSA: That gives a new sense to the idea of community, doesn't it? So, do you see any patterns regarding which material you have a tendency to rework and which material you don't?

FLOYD: Hearing your question, I think of two simultaneous answers, and I don't want to forget the second one while I'm answering the first one. I think we all have touchstones. We all have key moments in our lives or key places that we revisit, and sometimes we do it voluntarily while sometimes it's thrust upon us. Memories and experiences insist upon reclaiming our attention, so I know that I have these few core experiences that I have visited and revisited in my work, but I also know that material that I'm not aware of remains within the material I have written about—and it may come back as well. In other words, it's not just that I go seeking things out, but things come to seek me, and it's not necessarily a conscious process, and I prefer that it not be a conscious process. I'm working on an essay now about something I thought I was done with and had written about fragmentarily twice before, but it's clear now as I work on it, that fragmentarily working on it was the problem, and I had not confronted everything I needed to confront in the material.

> *I have come to realize that my memories and my past are not mine alone.*

MELISSA: I'm looking in the Blogtalk chat room, and Nancy Wait, from *Artists Ascension,* just posted a link to the menu from Toomey's

Diner and also a link to the poem. So, if anyone wants to take a look, it's all right there in the chat room.

Thanks, Nancy, for doing that. We appreciate it!

Floyd, will you read a passage from "Wild in the Woods: Confessions of the Demented Man" from your memoir *In the Shadow of Memory?*

FLOYD: Alright. This needs a little introduction. I'll try to keep the introduction under an hour. My wife, Beverly, and I got together in 1992 and married in '93. At first I was living in Portland, downtown, and Beverly was living in a little round house that she'd built in the middle of 20 acres of woods on a hillside in a remote part of western Oregon. So I moved out there to be with her.

I've been a city boy all of my life—was born in Brooklyn—and at the time I got sick I was living in Portland. I thought I belonged in the city, but one of the things I learned in the 15 years Beverly and I spent out there in the woods together was how badly I needed what I had come to out there in the woods with her. So here's the finale of an essay called "Wild in the Woods: Confessions of the Demented Man." The subtitle, "Confessions of the Demented Man" is in reference to the neuropsychological diagnosis of static dementia that applies to my brain damage.

Wild in the Woods: Confessions of the Demented Man

When the coastal wind blows hard through the trees and I see them swaying, I lose my balance, even in bed, because the damage to my brain has affected the system by which I hold myself in place. To retain balance is work for me. It requires a focus on what holds still. I need to stop thinking altogether to do it right. Seeing those trees every morning also reminds me that this is a land of second growth. The timber on much of our hill was harvested many years ago, and I live within the density of what grew back. It is a good place for me to live, a workshop in survival, in coming back from damage.

A person doesn't escape to a place like this. It's not exile; it's home.

I am not getting any better. But I am also not getting any worse. At fifty-two, after eleven years of living with static dementia, I have discovered just where that leaves me. Since I cannot presume that I will remember anything, I must live fully in the present. Since I cannot presume that I will understand anything, I must feel and experience my life in the moment and not always press to formulate ideas about it. Since I cannot escape my body and the limits it has imposed on me, I must learn to be at home in it. Since I can do so little, it is good to live in a place where there is so little to do. And since I cannot presume that I will master anything I do, I must relinquish mastery as a goal and seek harmony instead.

The short, grizzled guy living atop the Amity Hills looks like me and for the most part seems like me. He goes out in a storm to bring in a few logs for the wood stove; he uses the homemade privy balanced between a pair of oak when the power is out, which means the well cannot pump, which means the toilet cannot be used; he has learned to catch live mice in his gloved hands in his bedroom in the middle of the night and release them unharmed in the woods; he sits in an Adirondack chair reading while bees work the rosemary and hyssop nearby. He is my twin, all right, my demented self, wild in the woods, someone I did not know I had inside me.

MELISSA: That was beautiful and very inspiring too. I love how you talk about the land itself as a kind of blessing for returning back from damage. You were talking before you read the passage about getting to the woods and recognizing that you needed to be there. Can you talk about the importance of surroundings and location in a writer's life?

FLOYD: It's a bit of an abstract thought for me to try to wrestle with. I know that when you're sick there's this great temptation to focus on yourself and on this symptom or that symptom. I think of it as "Symptomania." You always turn inward and watch every new twinge and every change. It's tremendously narcissistic—long-term illness is—and it's dangerous for a writer, I think, to always be turned inward in that kind of intense way. So, one of the things that my surroundings did was to help me move outside myself. Now, of course, that led right back in as I began to remake connections, but it was something that I had not done before. I grew up in Brooklyn. We didn't have nature. I didn't grow up focused on the outside.

Since I cannot presume that I will remember anything, I must live fully in the present. Since I cannot presume that I will understand anything, I must feel and experience my life in the moment and not always press to formulate ideas about it. Since I cannot escape my body and the limits it has imposed on me, I must learn to be at home in it.

It took moving to the woods and slowing down, both because of illness and because of where I was, to begin to look far enough outside myself to see myself freshly again. And it continues. We no longer live in the woods. Beverly and I now live in Portland and right close to a river, and I learn a great deal every day just watching what the river does. But, that's a habit that I didn't learn until my time in the woods.

MELISSA: That's interesting. I remember reading about the circular house. Did you move to or away from the circular house when you moved from the woods to the river?

FLOYD: We moved away from the little round house in the woods. It was a cedar yurt. It was wonderful, with windows allowing us a tremendous view down the hillside, and we had a giant skylight. It was a wonderful place to live. But, we left that four years ago.

MELISSA: It sounds beautiful and unique, a neat place to live for a while! Okay—shifting gears now—I want to ask you a question about sonnets. You've done so many creative things with the sonnet—you sort of stretch them to their limits and then snap them back into shape. In one I think you even used the same first and last line. What it is about the sonnet form in particular that appeals to you so much, and do you intend to continue playing around with that form?

FLOYD: I'm very drawn to traditional forms, and particularly to playing with them and finding myself liberated within them. I think of the nature of my own personality, shaped as it was by my childhood and experiences in growing up. I need structure; I need order in order to feel my imagination freed. I'm just a person who requires order. It doesn't always have to be traditional, formal structure. I don't have to write sonnets. Half the poems I write are not in traditional forms, but even the ones that are in free verse have some kind of structure or organizational principle that has been discovered in the composition.

Now, why I'm so drawn to the sonnet, I really can't say other than I'm pretty steeped in Shakespeare, and I have always been drawn to the way a sonnet, particularly a Shakespearean sonnet, allows you to think and play with ideas within the form. My language is always very colloquial and loose within rigid structures. But the sonnet seems to be about the right length for me—maybe because I'm such a short person.

MELISSA: The sonnet lends itself to a sort of logical unfolding that I think is very compatible with the way you write. Do you feel like writing in form has influenced the poems you write that aren't in form? It seems to me like you create your own structure in the poems that don't have formal structure already. Does that make sense?

FLOYD: That's what I do. And it's all a process of discovering it as I'm doing the work. But I think working within rigid forms allowed me to become comfortable thinking in terms of the line and in terms of the development within what a poem allows. The different tools that poetry provides—the sound, music, meter, rhyme, rhythm— working in the traditional forms has enabled me to bring some of that to the non-traditional poem as well.

And I realize as I try to talk about this that I don't spend a lot of time thinking about what I do and forming theories about why I do what I do. In fact, I tend to shy from that like a ball player who doesn't want to think too much about his hitting because then all of a sudden he gets to thinking too much about it and he can't hit. I just haven't ever written any essays about how I write essays or about how I write poems, and I don't think about it too much. I just try to stay away from going there, in fact, which makes me a lousy interview, I think.

MELISSA: Not at all. In fact, I think it's one of the reasons that your poems flow so well. I've been studying poetry for years and years. I have an MFA in poetry and an MA in literature, and when I read your books, I thought to myself, "My God, I don't know anything about poetry." I thought I did all these years, and then I saw all the things you were doing so very naturally, and I was blown away. So, I appreciate what you're doing and I don't think there's necessarily a need to for you to analyze your own work.

FLOYD: I really have always shied away from that, and maybe one of the side benefits of being sick and disabled is I don't get out in the world that much, so I don't talk to a lot of people and get asked these questions all that much.

MELISSA: Okay. Could you could read "A Unified Field" from *The Snow's Music?*

FLOYD: Great. "A Unified Field" is from my most recent book, *The Snow's Music,* and I'm glad you asked me to read this. I haven't read this to audiences very much. It's a poem that uses the language and emotions from the fields of physics and astronomy, and I've always thought that this poem is about daring to love balance and harmony in the world enough to go look for it and even to foster it with the daring act of sustaining hope and of keeping faith in goodness. So,

A Unified Field

Because the night is clear and cold,
because the moon is new, and Mars
so close it seems to be in bloom,
because his mind imagines room
for wonder, he sees everything hold
together a moment under the stars.
He knows it will not last but loves
to see the world in balance, dark
forces merging with light, the drift
toward chaos stilled by the heft
of harmony. A unified field. Above
all, this is how he leaves his mark.

Now night bends toward dawn as light
toward color. Time is nothing we
believe it to be, but at the edge of sight
his faith sings beyond the things we see.
The torn fabric of the universe folds
over to heal itself. The beating heart's
energy echoes the brain's bold
leaps. This is when the mystery starts
to reveal itself, saying there are no
answers only better questions, new
beginnings there is no where else to go
No one else to ask and nothing left to do.

MELISSA: That's a beautiful, deep poem. I can't help but ask who the "he" is. Is there someone specific?

FLOYD: There is somebody specific, and let me say that it's hinted at in the acknowledgements in the front of the book. This poem, "A Unified Field," was commissioned by my alma mater, Franklin & Marshall College in Lancaster, Pennsylvania, upon the retirement of the college provost, a fellow named Bruce Pipes, who is a dear friend of mine. He was a physicist by training before he became a provost, and as he was retiring, the thing he was hoping to do most was to spend more time in his backyard with his telescope looking at the stars. So, when I was asked to write the poem for Bruce, I knew that he was a physicist, and I knew that he loved astronomy, and I had been thinking about these concepts anyway. It was almost as if the very forces that I was thinking about writing about had conspired to ask me to write the poem.

I read it at the commencement ceremony where he was given an honorary degree, and I received an honorary doctor of humane letters degree at the same time, so this was just a love fest. I mean, I was just ecstatic with delight getting to be back there on campus and getting honored as a recipient of the degree and being able to help in their honoring of Bruce.

MELISSA: He must have loved the poem.

FLOYD: Yeah, I think so. They gave him the poem printed on very fine paper, and I think they made five broadsides and gave him a framed copy that I signed, and he seemed to be happy with it.

MELISSA: I have one last question about poetry. You said in *The Night-Side* that poets should stretch their flanks and write longer narrative poems instead of always sticking to the shorter lyrical poem. Tell us some of the benefits of writing the longer poems. Even if the poems are not successful, the practice of writing them is beneficial, correct?

FLOYD: I think it's useful to go where you are not normally drawn, and the short poem has always been the place that I am most comfortable. Once I got sick, sustaining concentration for long periods of time, forming abstract thoughts—all these powers that would be useful in the writing of long poems—were gone. So, for me, trying to find a way to get past that and sustain something that seemed to be beyond what I was capable of became very urgent. In my case, the long poem has most often happened to be composed of shorter fragments that cohere. So, a six-page poem might be written in twelve different shorter sections that link together. But, I have also written a few poems, a few narrative poems, that were longer—several pages long—and for me, that's the reason I find it so attractive, because it's so difficult for me. And I want to see if I have material that feels like it can go on and on. I'd like to see what happens if I do go on and on after it.

MELISSA: Do you find that approaching narrative in that way is very different from approaching it in, say, a short story or a novel? I mean, obviously it's shorter, but what are other differences?

FLOYD: Right, it's shorter. I think the challenge is even greater in a longer poem because there is so much left out that to sustain a narrative across a poem is more difficult because it's even more compressed than trying to sustain a narrative in a novel or across the length of an essay of say fifteen or twenty pages. There's just less room in a poem.

MELISSA: I think you have some of the best titles I've ever seen— "Going, Going, Gone," "Gray Area," "Honeymooning with the Feminine Divine," "Wild in the Woods: Confessions of a Demented Man." Do you have a process for coming up with your titles, or is it different every time? I know my students have a hard time coming up with titles.

FLOYD: I don't. It's not usually difficult, and usually it emerges from within the work I'm doing—from the encounter with the material. I think because I write so slowly and work with fragments of my material for a very long time that, the title does declare itself as I am struggling to figure out where things are going.

MELISSA: That explains a lot of what I like about the titles—that they're so organically related to the material.

FLOYD: I've almost never had any problems with titles, with the one exception being the book of short stories that I am going to publish next year. I've written so few short stories, and as I collected

I did finally learn that I needed to take my time, and I needed to be sure that I didn't just get a poem done but that I had done everything that needed to be done to satisfy what the poem needed to be, that I discovered everything that the material wanted me to discover rather than forcing my way through it, ramming it into shape and, by golly, publishing it.

what I thought were the best from 35 years of publishing, I really had trouble coming up with a title. But, I have one now, and it's a title I'm happy with—but that was the hardest of all the titling—to come up with one for a book of short stories.

MELISSA: So, what's the title?

FLOYD: The title is *Cream of Kohlrabi*. Kohlrabi is a vegetable, speaking of organic titles.

MELISSA: Great. You said you have 35 years of short stories, and I know you started publishing in journals in the '70s, and you were having a lot of success with your poetry. But then you waited until the early '90s to publish your first book. You published all of these novels and other books, but you waited until now to come out with a collection of short stories. To me you are a model of patience, and I know you said you don't like to give advice, but I know people will want to hear if you have any suggestions about how writers can cultivate the patience with their work to wait until the time is right to bring it out.

FLOYD: I guess I would respond with an anecdote. I wasn't always smart enough to do that, and in the '70s particularly, I felt tremendous pressure to publish my poems. I was working a full time job, as I said earlier, and raising my child and running competitively and writing as well, and it got into my mind that in order to justify the allocation of time to the writing, by golly, I had to publish. It was a cost benefit analysis. It was cost-accruing and stealing time to write, so I felt that the benefit would have to be publication. So all I cared about was getting the poems done and out, and I published so much stuff in the '70s that wasn't very good, for that reason.

I know it's not possible to go around to every library in America and pilfer magazines that no longer exist in the world, but I published a lot of bad stuff, and it was because I was in a rush to publish. I did finally learn that I needed to take my time, and I needed to be sure that I didn't just get a poem done but that I had done everything that needed to be done to satisfy what the poem needed to be, that I discovered everything that the material wanted me to discover rather than forcing my way through it, ramming it into shape and, by golly, publishing it.

I guess my advice would be: don't rush. Enjoy the process of discovery in the act of writing. And make sure that you stay with it long enough to find out everything that needs to be included and then to remove everything that doesn't need to be included, and just don't rush to publish. I know it's easy to say once I have published seventeen books.

MELISSA: Yes, you have published seventeen books, but there was a long time when you were writing and not publishing. You may have gone crazy in the journals for a little while, but I think it's safe to assume that some of the poems didn't make it in to your collection.

FLOYD: My first collection, which came out in 1994, when I was 47, gathered the best poems from the first 22 years of writing.

MELISSA: You have been so prolific since then. It's really amazing. Sometimes two or three books a year.

FLOYD: A lot of that has to do with the vagaries of the editorial process. My first three novels were written before I got sick but not published until after I got sick. It looked as though, "My goodness. He got sick. Now look what happened. He's just spitting out one novel after the other." But, in fact, they were all done before I got sick.

MELISSA: I figured that was probably the case.

FLOYD: And that was the case with the poems in the first book, all but a few. I had never written any essays before I got sick in 1990. Nineteen ninety brought the first essays, two years after I got sick. So, it looks like abundant prolific productivity, but in fact, a lot of it had to do with a big inventory at the time I got sick.

MELISSA: Thank you for sharing this! You know, I don't normally ask interviewees about their family members, but I have to admit I am totally fascinated with your wife, Beverly, after reading your memoir. Can you talk about how her spirituality has impacted your spiritual evolution, and, in particular, I'm really interested in hearing more about Mother Meera and your honeymoon experience, if you would talk about that a little bit.

FLOYD: Can I claim memory damage?

MELISSA: Well, if you can't remember, I could tell about it from what I read. I'm kidding. No, if you don't want to, please don't, but if you want to, I'd love to hear about it.

FLOYD: It's funny—Beverly comes to all my readings, and has been so tremendously supportive, and people will come up after a reading and talk to her, and she'll say to me, "You know, the way you've written about me, I sound like Saint Beverly. I'm not like that."

MELISSA: She sounds very interesting, definitely.

FLOYD: She is a very spiritual person, and I was not conscious in my own self of the spiritual dimension until getting together with her and moving to the woods, and slowing my life down. And getting sick. All of these things turned me both more deeply inwards but also outward and opened me up to forces that I had not let in before. But, you know, beyond that, I really don't know what else I can say other than I sure feel blessed to have found her and to be with her.

MELISSA: I know you said at one point you thought of spirituality as a form of intellectual weakness. You didn't really take it seriously, but then, over time, I can see that evolution of how the combination of the things you mentioned has really gradually affected a change, which I think is very interesting. Okay, so you are going to ignore poor Mother Meera.

FLOYD: Well, it was a long time ago, and, yeah, I guess I don't really have anything fresh to say about that experience, but as far as that essay goes, it was true that before Beverly and I got married, she and her best friend had planned a trip to Germany to be in the presence of this woman, and we saw no reason for the fact that we had just gotten married to cancel the trip, so we just brought her friend along on the honeymoon and went there.

MELISSA: That's great. And to me, that's another one of the great titles: "Honeymoon with the Feminine Divine." I saw that, and I thought I've got to read this right now. It was just one of those things where it was in the collection, and I skipped forward and read that and then went back to the beginning and read the rest of the collection.

FLOYD: What was your reaction to it?

MELISSA: I thought it was wonderful—especially that you would be open to such an unusual and unique experience, and it sounds to me like you still figured out a way to make the honeymoon work since Mother Meera was only receiving visitors on certain days of the week, and on the other days you and Beverly would go off just the two of you, correct? So, it sounds like it was still a nice honeymoon, but you also got to have this unusual healing experience. After the fact, it seems you were a little skeptical about it, but, if I have the chronology correct, did you say that when you wrote The Night-Side, you had written three chapters of The Open Door?

FLOYD: Yes—it was more than three chapters. I may have said in *The Night-Side* that I'd had "three chapters" of *The Open Door* done, but once I got into the material, I realized I had written more. Seven of the chapters were already written and published as separate stories.

MELISSA: Oh, that's neat. And then you put them together as a novel?

FLOYD: That was the process. After we came back from our honeymoon I'd been given a writing residency at the Villa Montalvo at Saratoga, California, so we went there for six weeks, and that's where I pieced the existing stories and wrote several new chapters that made the novel *The Open Door*.

MELISSA: That's so interesting because when I read *The Open Door*, I just kept thinking, "Wow! This has a really pronounced narrative voice," and I know sometimes that's hard to sustain for an entire novel, and now you are telling me it was pieced together from several short stories, and it's so cohesive. I don't know how you did that. That's amazing.

FLOYD: It probably goes back to something we talked about at the very start, which was that certain material has always come up for me and insisted upon deeper investigation. A lot of the material, a lot of the moments that form the core of *The Open Door* were actually originally poems, which then became stories, which then became the novel, and, in fact, also ended up after the novel was written becoming key elements in the memories that form part of the *In the Shadow of Memory*. So, that was a case of poetry leading to short stories, leading to a novel, leading to essays, all being from the same material.

MELISSA: Switching gears a bit, do you feel like *The Open Door* reflects generational differences and attitudes towards child rearing, or do you feel that the situations in the novel are more unique to a particular family? The reason I ask is not as much because of the relationship between the parents and the children, but because the grandparents seem to just look the other way, and I just don't think that it would be the same now.

FLOYD: I don't know if that's true or not, Melissa. I don't believe that the novel deals with generational issues. I do think it deals with terrible specific issues of child abuse that were a function of a very sick dynamic between the main characters. And I think it is true, your comment, that the grandparents, the older generation, looked the other way. Within the context of that novel, that's what everybody did.

MELISSA: Yes, that's right. Even the teachers did.

FLOYD: I would hope that's not what happens nowadays because we are more conscious of these things, but I don't know—I hope it's not the way it was then. I can't speak to that. But, you know, that novel attempted to do something really weird. It attempted to write a comedy that dealt with child abuse.

The intention was, I came to realize, to keep the reader as off balance as the children in the book. You never know when it's safe to relax and enjoy the comedy of the book because something awful will happen in a heartbeat. I'm not sure it was a successful attempt or a successful novel, but that's what I was trying to do. I was trying to make the reader so uncomfortable that they would share this sense of a lack of safety.

MELISSA: That was definitely accomplished. It's hard to be funny with a subject like that, but definitely I saw the humor in the novel. So, you wrote about your Franklin & Marshall days, when you studied with the writer Robert Russell, in the essay "When the Clock Stops," which is one of my favorite essays of yours. In it you talk about reading Faulkner's *The Sound and the Fury* aloud for him. Can you talk about how it impacted you to read the whole novel aloud like that and some of the things that can be gained by reading something aloud as opposed to as just on the page?

> *...it brought me so close, so intimately close with what writing can do and how it is something that you do—both writing and reading—with the entire body—with your whole mouth and ears and gestures. It's an engagement of all senses—reading.*

FLOYD: What a wonderful opportunity that turned out to be. Doctor Robert Russell was the Chairman of the English Department at Franklin & Marshall College, and I was assigned to be his reader. He had, I think, maybe two student readers at a time, and once he and I got to know each other, and he realized some of the things I was interested in, he spared me having to read student papers and correspondence and assigned me to read books on to tape for him. This was before the day audio books existed.

The essay you're referring to is about reading Faulkner's *The Sound and the Fury* on to tape in a little closet room all by myself, and it was a fabulous experience. It was very difficult to do, particularly that novel, but it brought me so close, so intimately close with what writing can do and how it is something that you do—both writing and reading—with the entire body—with your whole mouth and ears and gestures. It's an engagement of all senses—reading.

And, I had to learn how to speak without any of the typical cues that fiction would give to a reader. He said, and she said, and clear delineations of time, and what was happening when Faulkner used of stream of consciousness, particularly within certain characters whose consciousness was terribly limited either by mental state or confusion or illness or whatever. He didn't provide you with a cue, so I had to understand how he was signaling a reader to not go astray and to know what was happening when and all of that. I had to find ways to do that out loud, and it was a tremendous education in what writing is capable of doing and the signals it sends. It was a full engagement for me with character and consciousness, as well as with writing and prose, as well as with performance.

MELISSA: I know you have an acting background. Have you ever tried to write a play?

FLOYD: I haven't ever tried to write a play, and I'm not sure I can even say why other than some very smart part of myself knows it wouldn't have worked out. We all know the story of Henry James and so many other writers who attempt to write plays. I just must have known somewhere inside that was not going to work for me. But I do know that my books, my fiction and nonfiction, rely very heavily on dialogue and scenes, and I think that probably comes in part from the work I did as an actor when I was younger, and I think it taught me a lot about how to shape characters economically.

MELISSA: That makes a lot of sense. We're about to run out of time. Do you have any upcoming events or publications you would like to announce? I know you have a couple of books coming out.

FLOYD: Yes, this first book of short stories, called Cream of *Kohlrabi*, which gathers sixteen stories, which I consider my strongest written over the course of the thirty-five or so years that I have been writing stories. All of them were written in the last fifteen years. In 2013, I will release my next collection of poems, which is called *Close Reading*. And, I'm, oh, maybe halfway through a book of essays, a memoir in the form of connected essays like all the other memoirs have been. I seem to be working at a pace that would suggest that the book will be done in two more years, maybe three, and I have been working on it for three years. So there you go.

MELISSA: Thank you. It was great to talk to you tonight, just a pleasure.

FLOYD: Thank you for thinking of me. So, for your listeners, and anyone else out there who is going to hear this or read about it later, let me just conclude by saying my daughter is the bestselling writer Rebecca Skloot, whose book, *The Immortal Life of Henrietta Lacks,* has been such a stunning success this year. Please go out and buy a copy of that and give it to someone you love because it will make their day.

Photograph by Marie McGing

ROBIN RICE

JANUARY 27, 2011

MELISSA: Our interview this evening is with Robin Rice, author, mentor, contemporary shaman, and founder of both The Awesome Women Hub and Be Who You Are Productions. Rice is the author of *The American Nanny, A Hundred Ways to Sunday, Venus for a Day, Shape Shifting Beauty* and many other books. One of Rice's clients has recently said: "Robin is a weaver of contemporary and ancient soul knowledge, a woman with a big picture, and a true thinker who is excited about life. She amplifies the stories of the GOOD and important, and works toward an even greater good and a larger whole. She is a voice in the wilderness."

I want to start by asking you about one of your concepts. Your novel, *A Hundred Ways to Sunday*, is such a unique book, and it's something that you refer to on your website as "living fiction." Can you explain that term and also a bit of what went in to composing your book?

ROBIN: Well, you know, there really isn't a term for the kind of books I write.

> *What I'm writing is fiction that tries to activate the soul.*

What I'm writing is fiction that tries to activate the soul. And so, as you read, and as you identify with the characters and their experiences and their awakening and their growth, you actually get drawn in to that awakening yourself, so a lot of people have very mystical experiences and enhanced dreams and feel like the characters are moving with them, which was by design. I didn't know how well it would work, but it does work really well. So, that's living fiction in a nutshell. I had to find a way to describe it because people were having these experiences, so it wasn't your ordinary reading to escape novel. But there wasn't really a place on the bookshelf for it. There wasn't any other title like that, although there are other books I would call "living fiction." For example, *Jonathan Livingston Seagull* or *The Alchemist*—some of the books along those lines really do also activate you.

MELISSA: I was going to ask you about other living fiction. You know, I have to say, I did have a mystical dream when I read the book, so what you say is absolutely true, and I'm wondering if you can unravel it. I know sometimes it's difficult with something like that, but are there any specific techniques you used that created that experience for the reader?

ROBIN: Well, there's the mystical side and the technical side. And the mystical side, of course, is going to be very hard to explain as a contemporary shaman. A lot of it has to do with the energy I'm embodying and evoking, and that's a very big topic. On a technical side, because I know you have a lot of writers in your crowd, I would say that I see it as one of my tasks to have on every single page a question that's brewing. I should say, this is actually a lot like life—that you either have a problem to solve or an adventure to follow on every single page. So, even if I solve an early, smaller dilemma, I've created a bigger one and am developing into those bigger dramas and bringing in the sensuality of every page, so you can taste it, and you can feel it. That's really what draws people into the story. Regarding really big life issues, the voice I hear in my head whenever I write says, "make it bigger." Sometimes I can't possibly contain how big it really is, so making it bigger, making it more archetypal, making it more relevant to anyone's journey, is also very magical. Then you can fit yourself right in there, and we hit things that everyone struggles with in a very deep way.

MELISSA: And I know, also, for me, something that added to that experience was the CD you created to accompany the book. Would you talk about how you came up with the idea of including the guided drumming journey?

ROBIN: In this book, Mary Margaret takes several journeys at the leadership of this character named Chief of No Tribe, and they're a pivotal part of her own growth and toward her understanding of what she came there to do. Those journeys became something readers wanted to actually take themselves, so I created this journey for them to go in more easily. You already know the characters. You know the setting after you've read the book. Sometimes shamanic journeying takes a lot of practice for people, but having the ability to go in guided by characters you already know makes it easier to get in. So, that was my intention. Later, I read from many people that you didn't need to read the book, and many people used the CD without the book, just imagining the characters however they imagined them. That works too.

MELISSA: I actually did it both ways. When I saw the CD, I thought, "Oh, I have to listen to this now." I listened to it before and after I read the book, and it was wonderful both ways. Also, at the end of the book—I don't want to give away the ending—but I think you know what I'm talking about...

ROBIN: Don't you dare.

MELISSA: If you read the book, you'll see that the book itself has a unique way of drawing the reader in, right?

ROBIN: Absolutely. What I didn't realize was that I was writing it on many dimensions and many levels. I kind of knew I was doing it, but by the time I was at the end I was like, "Wow, this is on so many levels at once, will it even work?" I was just surprised that it could possibly work. I had 12 or 13 friends who were all people I knew would either tell me the truth, or I would know if they were lying. They were reading it, and they were writing back within 24 hours saying, "I couldn't put it down. Can I bootleg a copy and give it to a friend?" You know, within a month, we had like 35 readers, before it was ever published, so that was very encouraging and indicated that I actually pulled it off—because I wasn't sure.

MELISSA: That actually makes me wonder about your process, because the plot is so intricately structured, yet it's also so very organic. Did you have a plan regarding plot when you sat down to write it, or did you just let it happen?

ROBIN: Well, all I can say is the end of the book is true. That piece is true.

MELISSA: Wow!

ROBIN: We won't give it away, but I had to follow the story in order to understand how I could possibly bring these concepts into absolute, everyday reality, so it wouldn't be pie in the sky and far-fetched, and so people wouldn't have to take a leap of faith. The main character won't take a leap of faith, as you know. Throughout the book she's like, "I'm not going there." So, I had to track it in that way. But, honestly, there were other things. I thought I was done with the book, and I made a discovery that ricocheted throughout the whole book. Literally fifteen minutes before I was about to hand it out to people, I went back and changed everything so that it fit. So, the process was very dynamic, and people think I am the main character, but I am absolutely not.

> *I thought I was done with the book, and I made a discovery that ricocheted throughout the whole book. Literally fifteen minutes before I was about to hand it out to people, I went back and changed everything so that it fit.*

MELISSA: That's good.

ROBIN: I know. But there are some parts that are really, really true, and I always say I write for me. So, I used it for my own personal growth. Some of the intense parts I used as my own growth, and sometimes it surprised me, because I wasn't expecting that. And I swear I quit the book 35 times at least. I just said, "I'm not doing this. This is too close to home. I'm not doing this."

MELISSA: How long did it take you?

ROBIN: That one took about two years. I have another one that took eleven years, and I started it before I started *A Hundred Ways to Sunday*. But, that one only took about two, thankfully. It was a very rewarding, full two years.

MELISSA: Do you ever work on more than one at a time?

ROBIN: No. I can't. I can barely do anything else when I'm writing. Like, for example, when I was writing my book, *Venus for a Day*, my husband, Brian, had recently come to be with me. This was a second marriage for each of us, and he literally would bring me food in the morning and at lunch and at dinner, and I wrote for eighteen hours. I actually lost part of my eyesight due to it. So, the challenge for me is to try to write this type of fiction at the same time as doing anything else. I'm not very good at it. I tried it with one book, and it's okay, but it's not as good.

MELISSA: It's wonderful that you can immerse yourself like that.

ROBIN: I don't think I could today.

MELISSA: You couldn't? No?

ROBIN: Not with what's going on in my life. No.

MELISSA: When I looked through your website and your books and your articles, your videos and everything you do, I just thought, "My gosh, how does she do it all?" So, I totally understand what you're saying. Actually, how do you do all of those different things? Do you have a secret?

ROBIN: People have been asking me that a lot lately, and I don't know, maybe you just get used to doing stuff all the time. I do work from early in the morning until I can't go any more most days. You could say I'm a workaholic if you really want to be pathological about it, but the truth is that this is what I feel the time is for. We are here now to do all we can. To usher in some kind of change in this world. And it's desperately needed, and anybody who can do anything I feel should get out there and do it. That just drives me, and I get exhausted—there's no doubt about it. I think when we first talked, I was taking five weeks off. So, I also do that. I do take care of myself, but it seems like I'm a sprinter and then I have to rest.

MELISSA: That makes sense. Can you explain to us what it means to be a contemporary shaman?

ROBIN: Probably not. But I could take a stab at it.

MELISSA: Do you think there's a distinction between contemporary shamanism and older forms?

ROBIN: I do. There are a couple of different answers. One is that shamanism has been found throughout all times and all cultures.

And so, what we are tapping into is a shaman today. Many people think more recent native Americans or more recent indigenous, and there's a lot of conflict in that because there are people who feel like the white people stole everything and this white girl is saying she's a shaman and they get deeply offended by that, and I understand that; I understand that actually very well and one of the reasons I say I'm a contemporary shaman is to distinguish myself. I am not a traditional shaman that you might necessarily think about from one of our indigenous cultures. I can't be. I was raised in the city. I can't possibly be that and I'm not going to take someone else's tradition and try to make it my own, so I have to find my own tradition. I have to embody what I actually know. But I also know that it goes way, way, further back than those stories that are currently causing the conflict right now, and I really believe that every person has a shamanic element to them as their birthright. I do not believe everyone is supposed to be a shaman. You wouldn't want to be a shaman unless you're called to be a shaman. It's way too hard. But I do believe we have elements of it as our birthright because we are human, and this has been with the human experience since humans began. So, that's where I use the distinction. First of all, to open up the question because it's an important question and also to honor those traditional indigenous people who were the traditional shamans that I could never be.

MELISSA: Great. Thank you. I want to make sure we have time for you to read something. Will you read the opening passage from "That Night with Julie," the article that originally appeared in *Natural Beauty and Health Magazine*? It's also on the Be Who You Are website if anyone wants to go and finish reading it. Is that correct?

ROBIN: Yes, www.bewhoyouare.com. It's under "articles," so it's pretty easy to find.

MELISSA: Terrific. Thank you.

ROBIN: So, you want me to just start?

MELISSA: Yes, please.

ROBIN:

That Night With Julie

"You're Robin Rice?" the young, dark-haired woman asked me.

We were in line, signing in for an open mike poetry reading at the local bookstore. I'm not exactly a household name, but as I am an author, some people know of my work. Given my own "off" mood, I was prepared to put on a polite smile. One look in to this young woman's deeply troubled face and I knew this was not the tack to take. You don't have to be psychic to know what that kind of face means. You only have to have been there yourself. This woman-child was on the edge of her own life, and looming toward a jump.

"Yes," I answered.

"I hear you know something about depression," she said, looking at me with both need and suspicion. Her name was Julie, and, as it turned out, her mother knew someone who knew someone else who had been depressed and come to me for mentoring. I've always been willing to share my story about overcoming 25 years of recurring depression, but this night I didn't have much to give. It was tempting to hand her my card, tell her to give me a call.

Something inside said, Talk to her. Now. Tomorrow may not come.

We both had our hot drinks, and our names were well down the list for performing our poems. We agreed to move to two comfy chairs

> *This was youth in its prime and beauty, yet with no vision, no sense of the value in living, no future to walk towards.*

and relative solitude. An eerie feeling came over me, as if everyone else in the store had disappeared. It was just me, Julie, and a lot of books.

Visions of my little brother, Ricky, flashed in front of my eyes. He had been where Julie was when he was 18 years old. I hadn't lived close enough to see the desperation in his eyes, and it was still hard to admit I had not heard it in his voice on the phone only days before his suicide.

My body trembled. Something in this encounter was beginning to feel like a possible redemption. Even though my life was already devoted to helping others, this felt different. This was youth in its prime and beauty, yet with no vision, no sense of the value in living, no future to walk towards. I did not know how to address such a travesty. I could only hope my best would be enough.

"You must be willing to recover your soul," I said.

She looked at me blankly. I decided to start again. "If you want to live a soulful life, which is the only way I know to truly relieve depression, you must be willing to be who you really are-to look at the world through different eyes than the ones you've been trained to use your whole life. You must be willing to drop to a deeper level of existence, a level that is pleading to you through the worst of your days, asking you to listen to it. You must be willing to look for the legend that is trying to be told within your own life." I took another deep breath, surprised at the lofty nature of my own words, but unwilling to tone them down. Something was unraveling in me. It was going to have its say.

"To live a soulful life, you must be willing to not fit in. Because if you are this deeply hurt by life at this young an age, you don't fit in. You never will, at least not in the usual ways. I'm sorry if that disappoints you, but we might as well be honest. What the surface level of life is selling you will never satisfy your kind. But that's okay. It's never satisfied a lot of the most amazing people that have ever lived."

Julie pulled a small notebook out of her purse and began writing. It encouraged me to go on.

"To live a soulful life, you must be willing to stand alone, up against what everyone and everything in our society tells you is right for you, and ask what your heart wants, what your very being desires. You have to be willing to love who you really love, not who you are supposed to love."

I shifted toward her, lowering my voice to deliver the greatest of secrets. "Let me tell you something. When people come to see me, I ask them who and what really turns them on, what calls them to their depths. Most often, they say they don't know. But I don't buy it. They do know. It is just that their answers are not on the "good for you" or "easily attainable" list. Or, they don't know how to get what they truly love without losing something else they think their life depends on. So they've shoved what they love into a closet and often forgotten it entirely.

"These loves are really callings. They are the pearls of great price we must travel to the ends of the earth for. But very few among us talk about that heroic journey anymore, so very few actually embark on one. If you want a soulful life, you must be willing to listen for that call, and follow it whatever the cost."

I saw a light sparkle in Julie's eye. I could see her rummaging through her memories, then finding something of worth. I didn't need to know what she found. I trusted it, whatever it was.

"To live a soulful life, you must be willing to encounter obstacles. We live in an age where people think that the smooth road is a sign they are on the right road—that if God has called you to something, but barriers arise, then either you have been abandoned or you must have gotten the call wrong in the first place. It's not so. These very barriers are also the hand of God, preparing you to receive the bounty. You would not be wise enough to keep what you find otherwise. It's worked this way throughout history and in every corner of the world. Every modern invention we have will not change those rules. Just ask Joseph Campbell, one of my closest personal friends."

"I thought he was dead," Julie remarked, surprising me that she knew of him at all.

"His body is," I admitted. "But his soul lives on, here in this bookstore and countless personal and public libraries across the world. To live a soulful life, you must be willing to make friends with your kind of people in whatever way you can."

"I never meet my kind of people," she said, her eyes flashing with both profound sadness and fresh-cut anger.

"That's my point. I don't meet them very often either. But they can be found here," I said, pointing toward the vast array of books along the shelves. "David Whyte is one of my greatest soul supports, though I've never met him. Annie Dillard, too. And Arnie Mindell and Thomas Moore and Rilke and Kipling and Krishnamurti. I tell you, Lao-Tzu and all his translators often keep me company late at night, when the 3 AM witching hour strikes me dead awake in an empty house. I don't have to have tea with them to feel their presence, to not feel so alone. They are my people. Time and space matter little to the soul."

Julie sighed. I knew she wanted better than that. I often do, too. But life is what it is. Real hands to hold are not always available.

MELISSA: Thank you. That was a great reading. I loved it on the page, and I like it even better now.

> *We live in an age where people think that the smooth road is a sign they are on the right road—that if God has called you to something, but barriers arise, then either you have been abandoned or you must have gotten the call wrong in the first place. It's not so.*

ROBIN: It's a very powerful story for me because it's based on truth.

MELISSA: And it's amazing too because it was an encounter with a young girl. How old was she?

ROBIN: I don't know, maybe 16, 17, 18. It's part fiction and part true. I put it all together to create a living fiction story out of it.

MELISSA: I think the lessons that can be learned from that article are, really, things we need to keep learning over and over. So, it's great for adults too.

ROBIN: I think we all need to hear that. That it's normal. That if you truly do have a deeper, soulful existence, there are lots of people who are going to feel this way, and you are not the one person singled out of the rest of the universe who feels this way. It's actually incredibly common for anyone with depth.

MELISSA: One of the other things that fascinates me about the article is the way you talked about how barriers are there to prepare us. Will you talk about what the barriers might look like and how they can prepare a person for their bounty?

ROBIN: Well, you know, we look at our young rock stars, and they're on drugs a lot of times. Why? What kind of maturity do you have to have to handle the world looking at you and saying that you have everything? You now have fame. You have looks. You have money. And you have people adoring you. You have everything that you're supposed to want, and you're not happy still, because they don't tell you that living soulfully is also on the menu. They leave that part out. So, you're supposed to be happy, but until you have developed that soul, and until you have struggled against yourself and found out what is true for you and what is not true for you, then all of that "wealth," and all the things that you want, they are going to feel empty.

MELISSA: Thank you. I'm going to change the subject because we don't have a lot of time left, and there's something I really want to ask you. In your article, "Spirituality & the New Feminism," you talk about discovering a new kind of feminism that's more freeing than the old feminism, and you indicate that the older form of feminism is based on more of a masculine paradigm. Can you talk about what the new feminism is and how you discovered it and how it differs from the more traditional branches of feminism?

ROBIN: Well, I took a real risk in talking about new feminism, and I tried to start out the article by saying, "Look, I know you paved the way for me." I'm very thankful for that, but, in my mind, the feminism that I saw still seemed harsh, and I didn't see myself as a terribly harsh person or feel like fighting. It felt like it needed to be something else. So, for me, it's about the spirituality of the feminine—not that there isn't a real fierceness to that—because there is, but it's a different kind of fierceness. I can't quite describe it except to say it's holistic as opposed to striking back and trying to prove something. It's more like an, "I know it, and I embody it" strength. I experience that through the many teachings of the goddesses. When I first encountered goddess mythology, I was like, "No, not that ooey, gooey stuff," you know? They're ugly, and they're not even real. I was very skeptical of all that, but the lessons they brought me about being a woman and the power of women just bowled me over. It made sense to my soul.

MELISSA:I want to ask a question that relates to the passage you read but isn't directly from it. It actually comes from your article "Living by Magic." In it you stated that in order to live by magic you have to open yourself up to grief. Can you elaborate on how a person can open up to grief and why it's beneficial to soul work?

ROBIN: You ask such big questions. It's huge. It's great. We all have grief. We all have this part of us, and we all resist it. It's like we're resisting a shot in the arm. Who wants to do that? But when we open to grief and just say, "Okay, yes, life includes loss, and I have some of that, and what does that mean for me, and how do I do that?" and we allow the things that have been stripped away from us to be stripped away and to be raw and to be vulnerable, then something new has a way to come in where we were hollowed out. In that article it mentions that grief hollows us out, so instead of being tight and holding on to make sure we don't feel that grief, we can open to it naturally, not to go looking for it, but to open to the grief that we actually have and say, "Okay, it's gain and it's loss, it's both, it's a cycle." Life is a cycle. Circle of life. Lion King. Basic stuff. But we are not taught that in our culture. We are taught that it's all good. It's all supposed to be great. It's all supposed to be light and love, and there's no shadow in here. So when we open to that, we actually have a possibility of living holistically and being imperfect and just getting on with our lives instead of forever fixing ourselves. My little brother committed suicide. I don't care what you say. I don't care what you do. You can't fix that. You can't bring him back to me. I don't care what story you give me. That is a part of me now. It is part of my soul, and I'm not devastated by it anymore, but it's the landscape of my soul. And I want it to be because it was mine to go through. I went through it. I loved him dearly. I still love him dearly, and I don't want to let go of that, and I want to heal from that. I don't want to pretend it's impossible to heal from that. I'm just going to be who I am because of it. Does that make sense?

MELISSA: Yes. Absolutely. That's an amazing answer. Thank you so much. I wish we could talk more. I have so many other questions, but we're out of time. Do you have any upcoming events or publications or anything else you'd like to announce?

ROBIN: I have lots of things going on. You'll find information on my shamanic offerings at www.TheContemporaryShaman.com, and my other work at www.BeWhoYouAre.com. You can go to www.VenusForADay.com and get one of my novels for free as a PDF. And of course, please join me on Facebook at www.facebook.com/BeWhoYouAreWithRobinRice.

ANTHONY LAWLOR

FEBRUARY 21, 2011

MELISSA: Good evening everyone. Our interview tonight is with architect, author, lecturer and filmmaker Anthony Lawlor. Lawlor is the author of the blog Dwelling Here Now and the books *The Temple in the House, A Home for the Soul,* and two newly released books *24 Patterns of Wisdom* and *Two As* One, co-authored with Sherrie Lovler. Jean Houston has stated that "The *Temple in the House* is a living temple in which the soul of architecture and architecture of soul are brilliantly evoked. The reader is magically led through patterns and proportions that transform the ordinary house into a charged place of spirit."

Anthony, how are you doing tonight?

ANTHONY: Great Melissa. It's great to talk with you.

MELISSA: It's fabulous to have you here. I'm going to go ahead and jump in with the questions. Anthony, it's clear to me from reading your books that you're interested in and knowledgeable about a wide variety of topics—mythology, world religion, nature philosophy—so many different areas. Will you talk about how these different interests have coalesced into your current practice of holistic architecture?

ANTHONY: Before I wrote this book, *The Temple in the House*, which was in the early '90s, I'd started a book entitled *Your Personal Style*. I got about halfway through before I realized it wasn't what I was here to write about. I said, "Okay, what am I interested in?" And I realized it was consciousness, architecture, nature, mythology, and, furthermore, that I had been gathering information for years. So over one Thanksgiving weekend, I actually outlined the entire book. For many years, I'd been interested in meditation, how consciousness affects form, the relationship between spirit and matter. All of these things, and all of their manifestations have always interested me.

MELISSA: That's amazing. You did that over Thanksgiving weekend? You outlined the entire book?

ANTHONY: Well, I'd been preparing for it over many years. I just didn't know it.

MELISSA: Wow.

ANTHONY: I just said, "What are you really interested in? What do you really want to do?" And I realized it was all there.

MELISSA: You mentioned meditation, and that piques my interest in how meditation, specifically, has impacted your practice of architecture.

ANTHONY: In a huge way. Most approaches to architecture deal with outer form and style and appearance. And even before I started studying architecture, I was interested in meditation. I traveled to India for

> *I realized that every designed object, whether it's a toothpick, a chair, or a city, started out as a thought, as a string in consciousness that was then combined with the materials of nature to form that object.*

9 months, and when I started studying architecture, I saw the real power of it for me was how those outer physical forms relate to the inner spiritual dimension of consciousness. It was about how form affects our experience in the world and how our consciousness shapes form. I realized that every designed object, whether it's a toothpick, a chair, or a city, started out as a thought, as a string in consciousness that was then combined with the materials of nature to form that object. So for instance, somebody has a desire to sit— the desire is there first and then they conjure the idea of a chair, so they go find wood or metal or some other material like that, and it's the integration of that imagination with the material objects that creates the form. I realized that every form in our human physical environment is an expression of our imagination, and we literally dwell within our human imagination. From the moment we are born we're in designed forms, so we're surrounded by form that has been shaped by consciousness.

MELISSA: That's amazing. As you were talking about the connection between consciousness and materials, I was thinking that one

of the things your work promotes is a different way of *being* in relation to the materials of the earth. Will you talk about the importance
of the kinds of materials you use in design?

ANTHONY: Yes, nature is not a static object. It's a living, breathing, entity. It has an intelligence too, so the qualities of wood are
different than the qualities of stone, which are different from the
qualities of glass or some other material. So, when we're designing,
we're really having a dialogue with the material. A great cabinet-
maker, for instance, or furniture maker, engages in that dialogue
with the wood and then creates a chair or a table or cabinets that
embody what that material is capable of. I always love this little
dialogue.

There was a great 20th Century architect named Louis Kahn who
would say: I ask a brick, "What do you like, brick?" And brick would
say, "I like an arch, because you put bricks together to make an
arch." And Khan said, well, what if you say to brick, "I can stand
between those two columns with a concrete beam. What do you
think of that, brick?" And he said brick would say, "I like an arch
because the arch brings out what brick can do." It takes it out of
just a lump of matter and shows how it can express its beautiful
shape of the arch.

MELISSA: I love that.

Now, in your other book, *A Home for the Soul*, you identify some
archetypal symbols for the functions of various rooms in the home.
Can you talk about some of these and how incorporating them into
the home can enhance healthful living?

ANTHONY: When designing homes for people, 90% of it is not about just the function of the home, the function being how big the rooms are, where you place clothes in the closet. Most of it has to do with our belief about what a home is. So people spend all kinds of money designing a kitchen that is more than just a function of heating food and keeping it cool in the refrigerator. There's that sense of the hearth of home, and every room in the house is like that.

In *A Home for the Soul*, I talk about making every room a little space for honoring the different aspects of the human mind-body connection so that the bathroom is not just a place to unconsciously stumble into and take a shower, but it's a place to honor the body and care for the body. For instance, the dining area is the place to honor that aspect of coming together for a meal and celebrating not just daily nourishment, but holidays and such. Every facet of the house, even the doorways between rooms, can be a used as a means to honor the activities taking place and the experience of being in that house.

MELISSA: I can definitely hear your mediation experience coming out in that answer. It's about being more mindful in a lot of ways. Can you talk about some specific ways people can implement this? I know you have excellent examples in your book, and we don't have enough time to get into all of them, but I'm thinking of such specifics as putting seashells in the bathroom to draw in nature.

ANTHONY: Yes—the kitchen, for example, is sort of an alchemical laboratory where you're taking the basic elements of fire and water and earth and air and combining them to transform these substances of food into nourishing meals. So one way to do this is to think of your kitchen stove almost as a little altar where you cook, and, so, you set it up with the utensils around as this opportunity to engage in the mindful act of cooking. The whole kitchen can be like that, so that the sink is a place for cleansing and cleaning, and the cutting area is the place for transformation. You can think of colors and materials and shapes that will support those different activities, so instead of just thinking of one color for the whole kitchen, you could have a cooling, soothing color scheme using blues and greens around the sink, but around the stove more fiery colors and material.

Just take a step back from your commonly held beliefs about the kitchen and say, "Okay, what is this kitchen *really* to me?" Also, memories from your childhood or from a movie you have seen or books that you have read can be relevant. There are all these wonderful images that go with every room in the house - the bedroom, the family room around the fireplace, your home office, your home meditation room. You can make these places of your imagination and places that nurture your soul, not just places to put your stuff.

MELISSA: Wonderful. Thank you. There's something you briefly touched on in the first part of that answer that I would like to have you elaborate on a little more, and that is the importance of what you call the *between* spaces and passageways. Certainly, I think a lot of people haven't thought about them much before, and you talk in your books about how to honor the importance of these passages with design.

> *You can make these places of your imagination and places that nurture your soul, not just places to put your stuff.*

ANTHONY: Think of the front door to your house or your apartment. Every day it's a threshold to either go from the sanctuary out into the world or to return from the world to your home. These are very monumental points in your day, and you can either unconsciously just stumble across the threshold, or you can treat it in a way that enhances and honors it. Now, people traditionally do this with a welcome mat or something like that, but think of all the experiences that happen in the front door. Your first kiss might have been at a front door, or going off to college, your first day of school – all of these memories.

Another aspect of entrances is that in every threshold we cross there is always some desire or hope and then there is always some fear of what will happen when you cross that threshold, so there are twin doors of hope and fear that border the gateway to a house, and one way of decorating or shaping a house is to embody those experiences in your own way. Traditionally, for instance, at the entrance to Notre Dame Cathedral, there's an arch, and on one side of the arch there's hope with all the saints, and on the other side there are devils, and they exhibit fear. Actually, they look like they're having more fun than the saints. But, the point is to show this duality and that by crossing the threshold of moving between those two opposites, you move into the unity of the sacred beyond that experience.

To translate that to your home—what is it that you hope for in your home and your life and for your family and for yourself, and what is it that you fear? And if you faced that fear and went beyond it, how would you feel more empowered by moving through it? So even if it's just a color, such as having the colors of hope on one side and the color of something more trepidatious on the other side, you can embody that experience for yourself.

MELISSA: One thing you mentioned in your books that really stood out to me was the idea of painting a door frame in your home a vibrant color to mark the passage and to call attention to crossing from one room into the next. It's certainly something I've never thought about before, and what an amazing idea that is.

I want to ask you a question now about your most recent blog, "Healing Space: New Architecture for an Emerging Culture," at the *Dwelling Here Now* blog site. You present a design there that just completely takes my breath away. I posted it on the *Tiferet* site earlier. People who commented at the site said they felt healed just from looking at the design, and I have to say I had a very similar experience. Can you talk about the design and also whether or not you have ideas for similar designs for the future?

ANTHONY: I created that design because I wanted to show a project that was developed from the approach of moving from the inner to the outer, one where the architectural form reflected the mystic experience of going through—in this case healing. So what I started out with before I thought about a building was the thought: what is the process of healing?

I thought, okay, the first phase is shedding, where you are just like a snake moving out of its old skin. It's kind of a breakdown phase where you feel wounded, or it's an emotional or physical healing, or some time where you just have to let everything go. So then I thought, alright, what kind of place would allow that to happen? And I said, okay, for the first room of this structure, let's make a place under ground, almost like a cave, a womb-like experience where you could just totally let go. You could sleep for days. You could cry.

MELISSA: Sounds heavenly.

ANTHONY: We've all experienced those times in life when we just want a place to let the world go, and to shed everything, and to allow ourselves to process.

So, next I had a middle level, a ground level—that was what I thought of as the second phase of the healing process, the creative phase. After you've shed all of the stuff and gotten away from the things you wanted to let go of, then there's the creative energy that allows you to start to heal, so I had a place for reading, drawing, and writing—for doing creative kinds of exploration, like journaling, and just exploring who you are after you've shed that wounding.

The third phase of healing I thought of as connecting that new creative phase with the world. So I put a roof deck that had instruments you would connect to. You would look at the path of the sun, the path of the moon. You would connect that to the greater pattern in the renewing process of nature. As you went through the structure, you would have the shedding, the re-creative phase and a reconnection with the world phase. So I thought of this at first, and then I started to design the structure, and it all came together around that.

MELISSA: I want to emphasize to listeners that the design is absolutely stunning. There is no way to really convey it by talking about it, so I really encourage you to go to the blog. It's so beautiful.

ANTHONY: Thank you. I do want to add that one reason I created the project and came at it from the way I described is that so many times we just repeat old structures and become unconscious and incorporate a kind of numb-

> *...so many times we just repeat old structures and become unconscious and incorporate a kind of numbness into our lives, so I wanted to create a structure that kind of woke you up when you saw it.*

ness into our lives, so I wanted to create a structure that kind of woke you up when you saw it. It's something different from what you see every day, but at the same time it feels like coming home. So that was also part of the design.

MELISSA: It absolutely does that, and it also feels connected to the natural surroundings. I mean it's what in your books you call *living architecture*. Do you have any similar designs, or is this the first one?

ANTHONY: I have some others, but I haven't had the chance to draw them up. My plan is to draw some others up and put them out there for people to experience.

MELISSA: That's great. Can you also talk about seed imaging, which you explain in *The Temple in the House*? It's such a wonderful concept. Can you tell people how it works? Also, I want to mention that in the book there's actually a whole Q&A for the reader to do a creative visualization. Do you have any plans to make that into a CD or something people can buy and listen to? I know I would get it.

ANTHONY: Well, I do have plans. So, yes, I am working on another book now, and with that my plan is to do CDs and videos because another advantage of connecting the whole consciousness to the spiritual dimension of architecture is that you can see it in three dimensions. Then we're not just talking about abstract concepts, but you can connect those elusive experiences in consciousness with tangible form of design.

MELISSA: I noticed in your film you did just that. I was amazed by how the images transitioned from one into the other in a way that really calls out the connections between the images. I thought that was beautiful. Going back a bit, though, since I distracted you before, can you explain seed imaging and how people can do it?

ANTHONY: One thing I noticed in working with people to design their houses and other structures is that what they usually lacked was some kind of common reference point that they could relate all aspects of the design to. I thought if they had that, then the design would be more integrated. Usually when people start a design of a home, for example, they cut out pictures, and they have a collection of a lot of nice parts, but it's important to have an integrated, holistic quality. So I came up with this idea of what I call a seed concept, in which you look at every choice in a design process—whether it's the shape of the roof or the placement of the kitchen or a particular door knob or the color of a wall—in the context of a reference point. So the seed concept is kind of the essence, the essential feeling, of the design.

How I work with people to get to that is a kind of meditative process where I have them sit quietly and then just settle down and become aware of their breathing, and then become aware of the essence of feeling in their heart. Then I have them do a little sketch or something that expresses the form of that essence. For instance, I show one seed concept in the book that's kind of like a point with rays radiating in one direction like a fan. This came from a project I did with some people. What resulted was that you entered the house, and everything was radiating like a fan from that central point of the door. So the design related to the seed concept, with all aspects of the design relating back to it.

My idea was to have a simple form you could relate to all of the design, and it could be anything. It could be a color, the shape of a leaf. It could be a pattern that calls to you, like a hexagon or an octagon or some other shape—anything—the shape of your hand or the human body or something that resonates with you.

If you look around houses, most people have some object or patterns that they have a connection with, and they might not even have a reason for that connection, but they feel a deep connection with it, and it speaks to something in their soul. So when they're making the decision as to what door knob they want and what dishwasher they want and practical things like that, if they relate it back to the seed concept, then everything will have that common thread that ties it all together.

MELISSA: Thank you. I'm definitely looking forward to the CD. Okay—now going back to the film, you talk in it about how global communication has expanded our awareness and how what were once seemingly different structures and belief systems are now more clearly perceived as multiple doorways to the same living temple. Can you elaborate on that idea and talk about how your travels helped you to develop this perception?

ANTHONY: Yes. About seven years ago I took a year and half off, and I traveled to many sacred places in the world, and the first thing that struck me was that even though the cultures were different, and the times and the structures were very different, they all had a common theme, which was the human experience. What is it that we're doing here? They all dealt with the questions of: Who am I? Why am I here? Where am I going? What is this place? What is this mystery of living in this world?

For thousands of years, in different regions of the world, different cultures were isolated. They didn't know that while someone was expressing something in a temple in India, someone in France was expressing the same thing in a Gothic cathedral. So what I saw as I was traveling around with the global communication we have now is that there really is a global consciousness developing, and a global culture, and that all of a sudden, all of these different temples seemed like so many doorways to one temple, which is this global living temple.

So what I saw as I was traveling around with the global communication we have now is that there really is a global consciousness developing, and a global culture, and that all of a sudden, all of these different temples seemed like so many doorways to one temple, which is this global living temple.

It's an amazing time we're living in. The whole effect of what constitutes a sacred place is changing.

MELISSA: The film demonstrates that so beautifully. We're almost out of time. Do you have anything you'd like to announce—workshops coming up or books coming out or anything that you would like to tell the listeners about before we go?

ANTHONY: Just go to my blog at dwellingherenow.blogspot.com and you can connect with the different things I'm doing.

MELISSA: Wonderful. Thank you so much for being here. Your books changed the way I look at things, and I'm definitely going to be making changes in my own home—I can tell you that.

ANTHONY: Melissa, it was great talking to you too. I really appreciate it.

BERNIE SIEGEL

MARCH 18, 2011

MELISSA: Our interview this evening is with Doctor Bernie Siegel. Siegel is retired from Yale New Haven Hospital where he was a Professor of General and Pediatric Surgery. He is the Academic Co-Director of the Experiential Health and Healing Program at The Graduate Institute, the founder of Exceptional Cancer Patients, and the author of numerous books, including *How to Live Between Office Visits*, *Prescriptions for Living*, and *Love, Magic and Mud Pies*. Wayne Dyer has stated, "Bernie is one of the world's most respected doctors. I would pay close attention to any prescription he offers." Larry Dossey has stated: "Bernie Siegel is a brilliant beacon broadcasting a message of hope. When high-tech medicine is supplemented with love and compassion, we have not only caring but also healing, which is what Siegel's message is all about."

MELISSA: Hi Bernie. How are you doing this afternoon?

BERNIE: Oh, I tell people never to ask me that.

MELISSA: Is it a long answer?

BERNIE: You know, I'm always sharing with the world that everybody is wounded, and I love holding up a piece of paper with

> *I mean it's the chemistry that then affects the genes. Your genes are deciding what to do. They're waiting to hear from you.*

a black dot on it and saying to people, "What do you see?" And a lot of people say it's a black dot, or other people say you're holding a piece of paper. But, I think every life has that black dot, and it's all about what we do with it. Something I love to do when I'm out and people say, "How are you?" is to say, "I'm depressed. I've run out of my anti-depressant medication, and my doctor is away on vacation, so I can't refill my prescription." I used to think it was funny, until my wife said, "You're not listening to the answers. They don't think it's funny." And I realized it was unbelievable how many people offered their anti-depressants. I mean from pocketbooks, their lockers, where they were working, all kinds of places. It helps you realize the world is wounded, and therapy can then happen when the wounded respond to each other. A line I love from Thornton Wilder is, "In love's service, only the wounded soldier can serve. Physician, draw back." That's a line from an angel telling a doctor he's not going to heal or cure him, and when the doctor asks why not, the angel says to him that what makes him a great doctor is his woundedness, so when many people say to him, "come into my house," they're saying, "you're the only person the family will talk to because of your woundedness." They're comfortable with him, and they won't let anybody else share with them, so he realizes that a lot of his therapeutic value comes out of his troubles and wounds.

MELISSA: Wow, that's a terrific story.

BERNIE: You know, your talk from *Tiferet*, there's a line in the column that says, "He who rejoices in the afflictions which are brought upon the self brings salvation to the world." Think about what that takes —to rejoice in your afflictions. But looking through various philosophies: Nietzsche said "love your fate." Joseph Campbell said, "Whatever your fate is, whatever the hell happens, you say, 'This is what I need.' " So, suddenly, the troubles become the teachers, and on a simple level, let me say to anybody that's listening, if you have a problem, it doesn't have to be health, anything in life—it could be marriage, kids, your job—how would you describe your problem to someone else? What words would you use? So, if you said cancer, divorce, or I lost my job, those are what I call diagnoses. We don't know what you're feeling, but if you use feeling words, then I would say to you, "How do those words fit your life?" I've been amazed at how much help I can offer when somebody with a severe migraine headache is about to be sent to the hospital and says it's pressure, and then her marriage is what fits the pressure, and she goes home 15 minutes later to work on the cause of that pressure and doesn't have to go to the hospital because literally her pain is gone, and she gets up and goes home. There are many other ways of putting it. A teacher would say it's a wake up call, a blessing, a new beginning, because they've used it like hunger. You know, "What nourishment do I need? What do I need to bring into my life to help me?" And then it becomes a gift and not an affliction.

MELISSA: I remember reading in your books that if you listen to what your body is saying to you, then you can get to the source of the ailment and what's causing it rather than just treating it symptomatically.

BERNIE: Yes, you know, pay attention to feelings. There's a wonderful line from a country and western song: "I want my heart to make up my mind." People do need to pay attention to feelings. Even in dreams your body will speak to you, giving you a diagnosis as well as what it would like you to do to take care of it—because the body is responding to feeling. I mean it's the chemistry that then affects the genes. Your genes are deciding what to do. They're waiting to hear from you. So, on Monday mornings we have more heart attacks, strokes, suicides and illnesses because the body is responding to how you feel about Monday. This is the part that has kept me doing support groups for cancer patients and others for 30 years. Because when you help people redirect their lives and love their lives, some amazing things happen in their bodies. It's not an accident when a so-called incurable disease goes away. There's always a story about how the person changed their life. One that made me laugh was a letter from this woman saying that she'd felt awful and even agreed with her doctor that she had only a few months to live. Then she listed all the things she started doing, from getting a dog to laughing more. It just goes on. But the letter ends with, "I didn't die. Now I'm so busy, I'm killing myself. Help! Where do I go from here?" And I told her to take a nap. I never seem to stop talking because I keep thinking of more stories, but how do I judge a good hospice? They have drop outs and graduations because people are getting their life in order to prepare for death and then say, "You know, now that I've straightened out my relationships and put everything in order, I'm feeling better. Do you mind if I go home for a while?" So, a recent study showed that patients who were put into palliative care did better than those who were not. In other words, the ones who were not in palliative care continued on with their treatment, but the ones who were put into palliative care ended up living longer because of the compassion they received and the work they did during that period.

MELISSA: I think one of the important things you talk about in your books, in addition to how people can heal themselves, is how we can help someone else who is ill. For example, if we go to the hospital to visit someone, what are the ways we can be with them that would be better for them and help them to heal?

BERNIE: Okay, if you've been through illness, you become what I call the native, so you're more help actually, and that's why the group support becomes a good idea. They're not getting a lecture from somebody who hasn't been there, and, also, studies show that just being there for people is important. I always tell people to do this experiment: go into your bathroom, put your hand in a bucket of ice, and keep it there

> *I always tell people to do this experiment: go into your bathroom, put your hand in a bucket of ice, and keep it there until it's too painful for you to tolerate. Then, surround yourself with loved ones and put your hand in a bucket of ice and watch how much longer you can keep it there.*

until it's too painful for you to tolerate. Then, surround yourself with loved ones and put your hand in a bucket of ice and watch how much longer you can keep it there. So, whether you're putting a hand in a bucket of ice or having a child or going through surgery, if you're surrounded by loved ones, you have far fewer complications and pain than if you're isolated and alone. So, just your presence makes a difference. The other thing I've learned is something from Helen Keller, who said that deafness is darker by far than blindness. So, the best way to help others is to walk in and say, "How are you doing? How can I help you? Is there anything you need?" and be willing to listen. If you only said, "Oh, I just listened to an hour of Bernie Siegel, so here— read his book, do this, do that," I say, "No. You are not helping." But if you walked in and said, "You know, I heard this fellow Bernie Siegel, and I got one of his books. You might find it helpful." And you put it down. You don't ask, "How many pages did you read?" the next day. It's presented as, "I care about you. Here's a gift that may help you." I'm the coach bringing something out that's within them, so they're literally going to do better than the person who says, "Oh, that book made me feel guilty because he asks you what's going on in your life, and I don't want to answer, and then he talks about drawings, and I'm not an artist." You know, that's the guilt, shame and blame that people grew up with. Putting it in a broader perspective, we remind parents to really keep loving them and keep showing up, to keep being there for them—because that will prove to them that they're worth something, and then they'll make choices that are better for them rather than being self destructive and feeling rejected and indifferent and like nobody cares. And, I think, if you're there for them continuously, they feel that and make a change that makes sense and that is health-oriented and not self destructive. I really feel the most significant factor in our health and our lives is whether our parents loved us. I mean, did you really feel loved by your parents? If you grow up with that sense, you have self-worth and will take better care of yourself. Statistics again show this—that the disease ratio by mid-life is about one out of four if your parents loved you and almost one hundred percent if you said your parents didn't love you. All of this is related to self-worth and self-esteem.

MELISSA: Wow, that's amazing. And I hear you have five children of your own.

BERNIE: Well, there's a punch line to this. These are my sense of humor jokes, but, if people learn from their mistakes, why do they have more than one child?

MELISSA: That's funny.

BERNIE: Within our house we communicated. Their line when I was becoming overbearing was, "Dad, you are not in the operating room now." They were reminding me that this was our home, and I was not the surgeon, not in charge of everything. My sense of humor, which they weren't offended by, when they began to drive me nuts, was, "Do you know why your mother and I will never get a divorce?" And they'd say, "Why not?" and I'd say, "Because neither one of us wants the children." Then they knew, uh-oh, he's getting to that point. We better calm down. But you know, there was noise, there was humor, there was love. They learned that you could be angry when you didn't like how you were being treated or wanted attention and you were still loved, and that's exactly the key in the household. Robert Frost has a line in a poem that says, "Home is a place that when you go there they have to take you in." And that's how our kids will always feel—that we may not have liked what they were doing, but we loved them.

MELISSA: That's wonderful. Could you talk about how your interaction with children has helped you to develop your life philosophies?

BERNIE: A lot of children have surgery, and what I learned, literally, was that the kids could get through anything if they felt loved, and I would tell their parents, "If you're there and loving them, they can handle it because the kids are living in the moment. They are not like, "What's going to happen in the next year five years?" Many years ago, one of our children had a pain in

We know from drawing blood from actors that if you give a couple, a male and female a script in which there is a tragedy happening—the woman's husband is murdered and so forth—and the two of them are interacting, their immune function goes down. The stress hormone level goes up while they're acting. If they give them a comedy, the opposite happens and it restores the immune function, and stress hormones go down.

his leg and told me at age seven he needed an x-ray. I figured he bumped his leg, and that's why it was hurting. The x-ray showed a bone tumor, and the odds of it being a malignant tumor were like 95%. It turned out to be a rare benign tumor but, before we knew that, before he had surgery, I was totally depressed, thinking, you know, he will be dead in a year. I was trying to get across to all the other kids and my wife that this was what was going to happen, and he came to me the day after the x-ray and said, "Can I talk to you for a minute?" And I said "Yeah, what is it?" Then he said, "You're handling this poorly." Now, that's a seven year old talking to his father. So I said, "What do you mean?" And he said, "We want to go out and play and have a nice day, and you want us in the bedrooms depressed and upset. Why can't we go out and have fun?" It was like he hit me in the head with a mallet. It was like, "Yes, you're right. Why don't we go out and have some fun? So, go ahead." That week before we knew it was benign really taught me a lot. You know, we've had pets with cancer too. They're not worried about next year. They're trying to have some fun, and believe me, they've fooled a lot of veterinarians. We had a dog with extensive cancer, and the kids wouldn't let me put him to sleep. The vet said, "But I've never seen a dog this sick recover," and I said, "Our kids won't let me." So, I brought him home, and what did I do? I treated him as if he were one of my patients. I mean I loved him, massaged him, shared vitamins and meals with him, and within two weeks, this dog, who had been literally lying on the floor and unable to move, was up on his feet and out the door with our other pets. He lived for a year, and it always stunned the vet because he had never seen anything like that happen. But it's something I was seeing happening in people, and I realized it wasn't just about people. It's about the relationship, the connection, and what it does to our chemistry. Let me just give two simple statistics. Cancer patients who laugh live longer, and studies say that they don't even have to hear a joke. I mean, if you just laugh for no reason, several times a day, you live longer. And to anybody listening, laugh for a few minutes and watch how you feel. My wife, during my lectures, used to do stand-up comedy, you know, one-liners like a female Henny Youngman, you know, teasing people. And when I watched the audience, it really impressed the hell out of me as a doctor, because everybody, after twenty minutes of laughing, looked five and ten years younger, straighter, and as if they were sitting up higher than they did after I lectured for an hour. Then I'd come back and do another hour, but I always pointed out to them: "How do you feel now versus twenty minutes ago?" I wanted them to understand that this wasn't just having fun. There were things happening to their chemistry and their bodies due to the laughter. Another study showed that loneliness affects the genes that control immune function. So people who are lonely are more likely to get anything from flu to cancer because of that lifestyle. And you know, you can't separate yourself from your life. This is what I try to get across to people and why I would ask them what's happened in their life. You know, some illness would occur, and it wasn't about blaming them but trying to see what could have made them vulnerable. Now, you know, if it's the death of one of your children, or a lost job, or a move across the country—those are all factors that contribute to health. We know from drawing blood from actors that if you give a couple, a male and female a script in which there is a tragedy happening—the woman's husband is murdered and so forth—and the two of them are interacting, their immune function goes down. The stress hormone level goes up while they're acting. If they give them a comedy, the opposite happens and it restores the immune function, and stress hormones go down. So, I'm always saying to people, "Act and behave as if you're the person you want to be." In other words, don't blame yourself and say I didn't do it right today. And your family, the people you work with, can all be your coaches, you know. If they see you deviating from being the person you really want to be, they can give you a little verbal queue and get you back again.

MELISSA: Those are clearly excellent tips. You do write a lot about how to behave like a survivor. Can you give some more tips on that?

BERNIE: That's something doctors should give to everybody. When you go into the office, they shouldn't say, "You have this disease or six months to live, or this is going to happen to you" because people aren't statistics. The word I use now is "potential," and I talk about what your potential is.

MELISSA: That's good.

BERNIE: You know, what I tended to do was this, again in the late '70s, I began to do a lot of lecturing and meeting people who I thought were dead, and I would say, "Why didn't you come back?" Well, you know, if somebody told me to be dead, what's the point of coming back to the office? But I realized they all had a story to tell about what they did in their life. Psychiatrist George Solomon, years ago when he was working with AIDS patients, came up with a very simple list that he said would help him determine who was going be a long-term survivor. He even lists volunteers. I mean, there were a lot of people when AIDS came out who were helping others with AIDS, and they were often asking me "How come I'm doing well, and my friends aren't?" I said "It's because you're giving love and helping, and it makes a difference to you."

But his statements were: Do I have a sense of meaning in my daily activities and relationships? And you know, that relates to the mortality rate of Monday. I mean, if you work, your life has meaning in it, and you will be a lot healthier and live longer. Well, I always say, find your way of contributing love to the world. So, it isn't about what job you take; it's about how to contribute to the world. Because people are everywhere, whether you are landscaping, plumbing, or a veterinarian, people are attached to what you're doing, and you have to really relate to those people.

Another one that's really important is: Am I able to express anger appropriately in defense of myself? And I particularly bring that up to the people who go to the hospital beds. I say, "Don't be a good patient. That's a submissive sufferer who is likely to get the wrong treatment." You know what I mean? They will walk into your room and give your meds to the person in another bed or the next room, and you don't say anything, so they don't discover their mistake. But, if you're a responsible participant, you question them; you want to know what it is, what you're getting, and why, and they may say you are such a pest, but, yeah, it could save your life. So, if you are not treated with respect, speak up. That's why there was noise in our house. When one of the kids said to me, "Are you getting divorced?" I said, "Why are you asking?" He said, "You yell a lot." I said, "If I don't like how I'm treated, I speak up." He said, "But the neighbors are getting a divorce, and they yell." I said, "No, I love your mother, and I love you, but I don't like how you're treating me." And that's the point I would make to people—that there is appropriate anger. So when people say to me, "You keep writing all the books about love, and you know you're yelling at me." I say, "I love you, but I don't like how you're treating me." You know, that could be in a store or somewhere else where they say they're going to pick something, and they don't. You know, I get upset. I have to say, over the years, I've become a heck of a lot calmer and more peaceful because I'm a healthier person. So, I'm not projecting my troubles on others. If you say the world is full of lovely people, then you are a lovely person, and that's what you're seeing. But, if everybody is nasty, bitter, resentful, selfish, that's you, and you are projecting that on others.

A simple way of knowing, if you're looking for a good doctor or plumber—it doesn't matter what profession—ask: "Are you criticized by the people you work with and the people you work for?"

And, for doctors I'd say "nurses, family and patients." And the good doctors say "Yes" because they're learning from their mistakes. They don't make excuses. So

> *Find things that let you lose track of time. I think that's the healthiest state we could ever be in. It's a total trance state where you're not aware of your body.*

express the anger and don't be afraid of learning from it, even if somebody is angry at you.

The next two tips are: Am I able to ask friends and family for favors and help when I need it? Because what I find is so often people get sick and say, "Well I don't want to upset my family." But you know, who is going to support you, who is going to help you? It's like what we talked about earlier. How can I help somebody I know who has got a life-threatening illness or accident or something if they don't talk about it? How do you know, and how can you help them? So, you need survival behavior to ask for help.

Now, the next question is the most important: Am I able to say "No" to someone who asks for a favor if I can't or don't feel like doing it? Now, why is that significant? Because, again, if you ask your family and friends for help, they can say "No," they have a right to say "No, I can't do it." And you also have a right to ask. Otherwise, you're saying "No" to yourself all the time. Nurses I know have had great difficulty in saying "No" when somebody asks them for something. It's that nursing personality. But I remind them that you're not taking care of yourself if you're constantly doing what you don't want to do, and your body is going to suffer. It will do you a favor and get sick so you will have to say, "No, I can't because I'm sick." Learn to say "No."

Do I have enough play in my life? Find things that let you lose track of time. I think that's the healthiest state we could ever be in. It's a total trance state where you're not aware of your body. You're doing something creative and joyful, and you know, a few hours go by, you look at your watch, and you go, "It's been fifteen minutes or a half an hour." Yeah, that's good for you. Because that's that wonderful trance state where your body is just not a part of you because you're involved in something else and totally focused on something else.

MELISSA: Didn't you say somewhere that your body doesn't even age when you're in that trancelike state?

BERNIE: Yes, in a sense. If you do something for three hours, look at your watch and say, "Oh, my God, I thought it was half an hour," then I think you are only half an hour older, not three hours older. There's a wonderful line. George Halas, years ago, owned the Chicago Bears football team, and I don't know what book I read this in, but somebody went to his office because someone forgot their papers there, and he said, "I see George, who is almost 90 or something, and he's sitting in his office and working." And he said, "George what are you doing here at your age working?" And George said, "It's only work if there's some-place you'd rather be." And that's why you want your heart to make up your mind. Where do I want to be? What feels good for me?

Another one similar to what I said earlier about hunger leading you to nourishment is that you don't get depressed about being depressed. In other words, if depression occurs, you will do something and react to it and get help so you don't say, "Oh, I'm depressed; it's not good for me if I'm sick and depressed," so you get more depressed, knowing it's not good, and it gets crazy.

Another is that you participate. You are the responsible participant. You don't just fill every prescription. The family says, "Eat this." And the doctor says, "Take this pill, or you are going to have an operation." You say, "Wait a minute, let me think about what feels right for me." So, you participate in it because when you do—I call it labor pains—in other words, when you are in charge of the decisions, you have far fewer complications. It always amazed me and confused a lot of nurses how I would do major surgery on people and they would wake up, and they would refuse medication and say, "I don't need it. I'm a little sore; that's all." And the nurses kept saying, "They're refusing. They're refusing." And I would say, "They don't have pain. That's why." It's a different statement from they are refusing medication. It's about, "I am not in pain." So eventually, a lot of them were called Siegel's crazy patients, but that was an affectionate term, if you know what I mean.

MELISSA: Yeah, I do.

BERNIE: They would be having surgery, radiation, chemotherapy, and not having trouble and you know some of the other doctors would say, "Is my machine broken? Weren't there any drugs in them? Oh, it's Siegel's patient. We understand now why you're not having trouble." It's like with drawings: Some people draw the devil giving them poison as a treatment, and somebody else draws it as a gift from God. So, you can see why there's an enormous difference.

The last question is, "Am I living a role to the detriment of my own need?" And for men, I saw this over and over. "I can't work. What's the point of living?" These men, who were sitting in a room with their wife and children, were literally saying, "I can't work. What's the point of living?" And I pointed out there was a family they might have wanted to think about, and they would say, "Oh, I didn't think of that." So, if you were just a wage earner, and you couldn't earn money anymore, it would be like, "Okay. I should be dead." And for the women, I try to point out that what keeps them alive longer than men is their relationships. But that shouldn't be the only reason you're alive. You have to have a relationship with yourself. Because I have seen women stay alive while their kids grew up and then die, and I'm talking about 20 years later, they die of a cancer that didn't show up for 20 years, and then, suddenly, Boom! The kids are gone. Because their statement was, "I can't die until you're all married and out of the house." Well, they are all out of the house, and then it's okay to die? I would like her to be one of her kids too. Why don't you have a life now and enjoy yourself?

MELISSA: That's a great way of putting it—to be one of your kids.

BERNIE: Just remember, I added three questions just to find things out about people so they could know themselves. So, let's say I walk up to somebody and say, "Hey, I'm taking you out to dinner. What do you want?" If they're in touch with their feelings, they always answer immediately. But, if they stand there looking at me, thinking, I wonder what he likes or he didn't tell me how much money he's willing to spend, you know, and they just stand there looking at you—I say, "What's taking you so long?" Because kids will scream at you in two minutes or a second where they want you to take them. But I say to them, "Look, you haven't been through anything, you know, a crisis, a major loss or life-threatening illness. You're busy thinking. I want you to answer how you feel and pay attention to that" and sometimes I will also say, "How would you introduce yourself to God?" I want them to understand that they are divine stuff. If you say, "Oh, I'm a doctor," God will know who you are, but, if you're willing to say to God, "I'm your child" or, "It's me," God will say, "Hey! Come on in." And that's a very different message that you feel good about yourself.

MELISSA: Well, thank you so much. We're running out of time, and I just wanted to find out before we end if you have any publications coming out, or lectures, or anything you'd like to announce.

BERNIE: Well, first of all, I love that sentence: "We're running out of time," and I want everybody to remember you are going to run out of time, so enjoy your lifetime. Okay? Spend more time with the things and people you love and who love you and less with those who don't because time isn't money; it's everything. Also, we have a book that will be out in the fall of 2011 *A Book of Miracles: Inspiring True Stories of Healing, Gratitude, and Love* that is literally about miracles. And when I say that, I don t mean that everything is unexplainable, but just the wonderful things. Elisabeth Kubler-Ross used to say, "There are no mistakes, no coincidences. All events are blessings given to us to learn from." Jung's statement is that the future is unconsciously prepared long in advance and therefore can be guessed by clairvoyance. So, yes, some of them you would call a miracle in terms of disease, but others are just things that happened in people's lives that aren't coincidence. And how wonderful they are! But I think you get yourself into that quiet mind—the still pond is a symbol I use to everybody. You know yourself and your reflection when there's no turbulence. And a book that came out a little while ago was Faith, Hope and Healing. After each story is my reflection of what it teaches us—because each one is an inspiring story from people living with cancer.

MELISSA: Yes, I actually looked at that earlier in the week. It's a wonderful book. Thanks so much.

BERNIE: My pleasure, Melissa.

ARIELLE FORD

APRIL 18, 2011

MELISSA: Our interview this evening is with Arielle Ford. Arielle Ford is a nationally recognized publicist and marketing expert, producer, author, and consultant. She has enormously facilitated the rapid growth of the self help and human potential movement in the U.S. and is a founding partner of the Spiritual Cinema Circle. She is the author of seven books, including the popular *Hot Chocolate For The Mystical Soul* series. Her latest book, *The Soulmate Secret: How To Manifest The Love of Your Life with the Law of Attraction*, was released in January 2009. Marianne Williamson says of *The Soulmate Secret*, "Arielle Ford provides a beautiful way to let go of any hurts of the past and bring new love into your life today. Practical, inspiring, and hopeful, *The Soulmate Secret* leaves even the most cynical about love ready to find a soulmate." Michael Bernard Beck-with says, "Arielle Ford, in inspiring and encouraging terms, offers from her direct experience how to prepare in consciousness, heart, and spirit to magnetize, recognize and respond to the soul's call for an authentic, conscious love relationship."

MELISSA: In *The Soulmate Secret* you apply the Universal Law of Attraction to the task of finding a soulmate. Will you talk about what we mean when we say "Law of Attraction" and why the principles work for finding love?

ARIELLE: The Law of Attraction states that we draw to us the people, places and experiences that match our state of being. So, if our state of being is: I'm a loving, kind, wonderful person, who deserves to have romance and love in his or her life, then that's the experience you will begin to have. If your experience is: I'm unlucky in love, I'm a loser, I'm unlovable, nobody's a match for me, then that's what you will attract.

So, really, your thoughts and your emotions draw to you what you are putting out there. It's a really hard concept for a lot of people to get because what happens is people get into this state of wanting and yearning: "Oh, I want love, I want love, I need love," and what happens for them is they keep drawing in the experience of more wanting.

So, when you're working with the law of attraction, what you want to do is put yourself in a state of knowing, trusting, and believing that the one you have asked for is already yours. This requires that you become an emotionally mature adult and manifest beliefs, and that's the hard part for people because they either don't understand or don't have the discipline to manage their thoughts and emotions. So, just know that what you're thinking and what you are feeling is magnetic and powerful, and if you don't like what's in your life, you need to change the way you're thinking and feeling.

The great news is that you can "fake it to make it." You just have to make the time to do it. So, one of the exercises that I share with people is to begin living "as if." So, if I said to you, "Let's just pretend for the next five minutes that you know with absolute certainty that your soulmate is on the way," how would you feel inside?

MELISSA: It would be a wonderful feeling.

ARIELLE: So, what if you started spending time every day feeling like that—closing your eyes, sitting, and just wrapping yourself in those feelings? What if you thought, oh, my soulmate, the one I'm looking for, is looking for me and is on the way?

> *So, just know that what you're thinking and what you are feeling is magnetic and powerful, and if you don't like what's in your life, you need to change the way you're thinking and feeling.*

Spend time feeling it and start trusting and believing that it's real. That's how you magnetize love into your life. So, there are people out there who do visualizations, and they spend a lot of time thinking about what he looks like or what she looks like or how things are going to look. But, that's not going to get you where you want to go. You want to spend time feeling what you are going to feel like when that person is here and put it in the present tense. So, I call these "feelingizations."

MELISSA: I was just about to say that's a different concept, a different way of looking at the Law of Attraction, that is, I think, a unique tool in The Soulmate Secret. Is it a concept you came up with— "feelingizations"?

ARIELLE: Well, really, what I did was to just properly name it, because if you study with the masters who talk about visualization, they talk about the importance of feeling and knowing that what you ask for is already yours. But they call it a visualization, and people sort of skip over the feeling part, so I just renamed it "feelingization" because it's a more accurate term.

MELISSA: It's interesting that renaming it makes it more poignant and powerful and causes us to conceptualize it differently.

ARIELLE: Yes, exactly.

MELISSA: One of the things you talk about is clearing out physical space and unhooking emotionally from the past. Can you explain why these are important steps for attracting a soulmate, and can you guide us to some of the ways a person can accomplish clearing that emotional and physical space?

ARIELLE: Let's start with the emotional part of it. When we're intimate with another human being, we leave our energy in them and on them and they on us, so, when you're no longer with that person, even though physically it appears you are apart, you're still connected energetically until you cut the cord. There are invisible energetic cords that tie us together. So, there are lots of different ways to get unhooked. Probably the easiest way is to hire an energy worker who is really proficient, but another way you could do it is by taking a salt bath.

All you need to do is fill up a bath tub with warm water, add an entire container of table salt, soak in the tub, and then, as you let the water drain out, continue to sit in the tub, and, with your imagination, see all the energy from your ex-lover go down the drain with the dirty water. It's a fun process. Then you stand up and take a long, hot, sudsy shower. Shampoo your hair. Really get all the salt off of you and dry off with clean towels.

You can repeat this process as often as necessary, or, if you live by the ocean, a dip in the ocean can do the same thing. It's a really important process. Now, what could happen in the process of doing that is you may get a call from that person immediately or within 24 hours, because they will energetically feel you slipping away. They won't consciously know that's what happened, but chances are they will call to reconnect to throw their energy back on you. You may want to plan to take several salt baths.

The same thing happens in your home. If your ex-lover spent a lot of time in your home, they left a lot of energy everywhere, and you want to clear it out. So, again you can hire a professional energy worker or feng shui person to come and do it, or you can do it yourself. There are a couple of different methods I recommend. One is a Native American technique of "smudging" where you burn sage, and you take the smoke from the sage and put it over the door jambs and through the windows and in the closets, and you let the smoke from the sage purify and change the energy. Now, if you don't like the smell of sage, you won't want to do that.

Another way I have done it is on a nice, sunny day, open all the doors and all the windows, and take out a broom, and with your imagination, sweep their energy out all the doors and out the windows so that you are literally moving their energy out. And then to further prepare your home and your space for somebody, you want to clear out any clutter, so you want to move any mementos, photos, or keepsakes from the past relationship. You don't necessarily need to throw them away, but you do need to put them away.

Put them in storage. Put them in the garage. But take them away from your vision and anybody else who would be coming into your house, because the last thing you want to do when you're meeting somebody new is have them roaming around your house going, "Oh, who's this in the photo with you?" and "When were you in Greece?" and suddenly you're having a conversation about your honeymoon from 15 years ago. It's just not conducive to new love. So, those are two of the ways you want to clear the energy of your home. And even if you're thinking, "Oh, I'm never going to live in the place that I live now with my future soulmate," you still need to do that because chances are they're going to come visiting, and you want to be energetically prepared for them.

MELISSA: One of the things that I loved from the book is your statement that "the universe hates a void." So, in essence, if you're clearing that space, you're also opening it for someone else to come along, right?

ARIELLE: Absolutely. So, that's another reason to do all these things. I'm sure you've noticed whenever you cleaned out your closet and got rid of old clothes the first thing that happened is new clothes came in, right? Isn't that weird how that happens?

MELISSA: It wants to be full.

ARIELLE: Exactly.

MELISSA: Okay, so one of the things you really empha-size in The Soulmate Secret is that it's important to be very clear about what we're seeking when we imagine our soulmates. Can you explain why the clarity is so important, and what could happen if we don't have clarity?

> *If you aren't clear about the traits and qualities you want this person to possess, how can God, Goddess, or whoever you believe in deliver something to you?*

ARIELLE: Well, we talked already about how powerful your thoughts and emotions are, so just think about it this way: If you walked into Starbucks, and you said to the person behind the counter, "I need a tall, decaf latte. No, I think I want regular coffee with half and half. No, I think I want a half-caffeinated, half-decaf with low fat soy milk with sugar. No, better give me Splenda." You know, the poor person behind the counter doesn't know what to give you. You just asked for nineteen different things.

Think of placing an order in the universe for your soulmate. If you aren't clear about the traits and qualities you want this person to possess, how can God, Goddess, or whoever you believe in deliver something to you? So, you know, this is where being an emotionally mature adult comes in useful once again, because at this point, you want to do a little bit of research on yourself. Look back at your last several relationships. What did you like about some of these people that you would like to have as a feature, and what didn't you like, and, let's say your last boyfriend was a cheating, lying, unemployed, scumbag, okay? You will not want to put on your list that you do not want a cheating, lying, unemployed scumbag. What you can do is write positive statements. For example, "My soulmate will be an honest, loyal, monogamous, gainfully employed, kind, loving, compassionate, joyful, fun, person." So, by going to your past, you can figure out the future.

MELISSA: Frame it as a positive statement about what you want.

ARIELLE: Right. You need to put everything in a positive light. It's very easy to do. I could never be with a smoker. I'm actually allergic to tobacco. So, rather than putting on my list that I cannot be with a smoker, I put on my list, "My soulmate will be into health and fitness" because a healthy, fit person, of course, would not choose to smoke.

MELISSA: Now that we've asked for our soulmate, something I'm sure people will wonder is how to recognize when they meet their soulmate and what the difference is between a soulmate and non-soulmate relationship.

ARIELLE: That's a really good question. Well, there are two parts to that. One of the benefits of having a soulmate wish list is that when you meet somebody, and you feel that there's chemistry and compatibility and good communication, and you enjoy being with them, you can also look back at your wish list and see if they are lining up, if the major parts of this list are lining up with who you are seeing. Now, you won't always recognize a soulmate right away. Some people do, but it's very rare. So, the things you want to look at are chemistry, compatibility, communication, and shared vision for the future.

In some cases, you may not know for a long time whether or not they are your soulmate. I have one friend who is a dating expert. He didn't recognize his wife as a soulmate. They have been married for eighteen months, but he knew beforehand that they had a great time together, that they wanted the same things in life, that there were enough positives that he was willing to make a commitment, and eighteen months into the marriage he woke up one morning and it finally occurred to him that, yes, she was his soulmate. That's usually the case. But there are many, many pieces to it.

Since you are the designer of your life, you get to co-create your life with the universe. Then you need to ask for the heart traits and qualities that are going to give you long-term happiness. And these heart trait qualities and values are different than a laundry list of physical traits. So, if you are an ordinary woman of ordinary intellect, living in the middle of the country, it is not reasonable for you to be asking for George Clooney. But, what is reasonable to be asking for is somebody who is a match for you. Loving, kind, compassionate, committed, open-minded—whatever it is for you. If you have a certain passion—like I have a lot of friends who are passionate about animal rescue, they live to help animals—well, then certainly that's going to be on your list, because the last thing you want to do is get connected with somebody who is allergic to cats or doesn't like birds or is afraid of dogs. Or, you are a total fitness buff and you're always participating in triathlons, you don't want to randomly end up with a couch potato.

You want to think about what the traits and qualities are, and what your lifestyle together is going to look

> *Since you are the designer of your life, you get to co-create your life with the universe.*

like. You need to decide right now: Are children important to me? Do I want to have children? Am I willing to accept somebody who already has children? Or, in my case, I knew that I never wanted to have children nor did I want to raise anyone else's children. So, that was something that was very clear for me—that I was going to manifest a soulmate who was completely content with a child-free life, because, I was not going to compromise on that. We have sixteen nieces and nephews, and we love them, but my husband and I were in agreement from day one, and that was one of the ways I knew he was my soulmate.

MELISSA: I remember reading about that in the book. It sounds like it was such a wonderful moment when you were driving along and said, "You know, I don't want children." And he said, "That's how my last relationship ended. I don't want children either." I guess it's just so important to be clear on those things.

ARIELLE: Exactly.

MELISSA: There's a tool you share in The Soulmate Secret called treasure mapping, which I had never heard of before, and I just thought it was wonderful. Will you explain that concept and how it works?

ARIELLE: A treasure map is a visual representation of the future you're creating. So, after you've done your soulmate wish list, it makes sense to cut out pictures and words and images and photographs from magazines and then collage them onto a piece of poster board so you're actually creating this vision of the life you are generating.

It's something you can look at as many times a day as you wish to stick those images in your head as a reminder that this is what awaits you in the future. So, they are lots of fun to do, and several people who read The Soulmate Secret, who are now happily married, told me that what they did was to take a picture, a photograph, of their treasure maps and make it the wallpaper for their laptops and iPhones so they were constantly looking at their treasure maps. So, that's something else that I recommend.

MELISSA: What a great idea. It keeps it at the forefront of your mind. Now, you just mentioned some successes, and the book has so many success stories, as does Hot Chocolate for the Mystical Lover. Will you talk about the importance of sharing these kinds of stories and maybe highlight one or two of your favorites?

ARIELLE: You know, one of the things I find happening is that people get stuck in old beliefs around love, and the beliefs can be something like: I'm too old, I'm too fat, I'm too broke, I'm too damaged, or, one of my favorites is: all the good ones are taken.

I find that sharing stories about other people who have manifested love is very inspiring to people. For instance, my mother-in-law, Peggy, was married for 55 years, and then she was a widow for five years, and then at the age of 80 she called me and told me she was ready for a new relationship. Can you imagine? I explained The Soulmate Secret process to her. I just want to let people know that if they want to know more about this story they can go to www. soulmatesecretbook.com or www.soulmatesecret.com, either one. So, three weeks later, she called me up and told me she had a date.

I asked her how that happened, and besides doing *The Soulmate Secret* steps, she also had a friend get her on to match.com, because she doesn't know how to work a computer. There were three men over the age of 80 who were on match.com. One of them was a man named John, who was a retired lawyer like her dear departed husband, and her friend emailed John with Peggy's phone number. Well, John called her, and they spoke for five hours, and then they went out for lunch, and lunch lasted three hours, and within a short amount of time, John proposed.

They were happily in love, but Peggy didn't want to get married again because she had already been married, so they moved in together and they were just like teenagers in love. They couldn't be happier, and they lived together for three and a half years until last summer when John passed away at the age of 87. So, you could tell me you are too old. Peggy was old. She was 80 when this happened. Or, you could tell me you are too fat. Peggy has never been a thin woman. If you want to see a picture of Peggy and John, go to www.soulmatekit. com, and you will see a really cute picture of them. But, none of that is true. People just make up these stories in their heads, and they live like it's true, and then it becomes true for them because that's what their belief is.

MELISSA: Well, I want to make sure before we run out of time we get to hear a little bit about your next book that's coming out. Tell me if I'm saying this correctly, *Wabi Sabi Love*. Is that correct?

ARIELLE: It's coming out in January 2012. It's called *Wabi Sabi Love: Finding Perfect Love in Imperfect Relationships*, and it's based on the ancient Japanese art form which is

> *... to look and see who they truly are and how to find the good in what they're doing.*

known as wabi sabi, which finds beauty and perfection in imperfection.

The book is about finding the beauty and perfection within the cracks of yourself and the cracks of your beloved. It's a really sweet book with lots of true people, real people stories, and exercises on how to go from what I call annoyed to enjoyed. So, the things that may bother you about your partner we have fixes for, and a lot of it is just a shift in perception where we are seeing somebody as wrong or different as opposed to putting on a different lens to look and see who they truly are and how to find the good in what they're doing.

Now, I just need to make one caveat here. This in no way means that you should put up with abusive or destructive behavior. This is not a pass for bad behavior. This is for the little things in life that drive us all crazy. The way people squeeze the toothpaste, or they leave the seat up, or they can't make a decision, or, you know, they are sloppy in a particular area. You could spend your whole life trying to change them or you can make life easier for both of you and learn to love and accept their little quirks and behaviors as part of the greater good and greater whole of who they truly are.

MELISSA: Wow! That's beautiful. What a wonderful service to people who read that book. We're close to running out of time, and I'd like to know if you have any upcoming events, other publications, or anything you'd like to announce that I don't know about.

ARIELLE: Yes, thanks. I'd suggest that you go to www.soulmatesecret.com where you can sign up for my free, weekly newsletter or you can find me on Facebook at www.facebook.com/soulmatesecret. And lastly, if you are very serious about wanting to manifest a soulmate, check out my home study at www.soulmatekit.com.

MARC ALLEN

MAY 19, 2011

MELISSA: Our interview this evening is with Marc Allen. Allen is a musician, composer, internationally renowned author, and president and publisher of New World Library. His latest composition is a soaring, orchestral work called Awakening, and his first instrumental album, Breathe, has now sold nearly 100,000 copies and has been named a "New Age Golden Oldie" by NAPRA. His most recent book, *The Greatest Secret of All*, guides the reader in unraveling the secrets of happiness, inner peace, ease, and fulfillment. Best-selling author Gay Hendricks says of *The Greatest Secret of All*: "It is a wonderful contribution to humanity. It gives us the key to a life well lived."

Hi Marc. Can you start by briefly sharing the story of how you changed your life path at the age of 30?

MARC: I love telling that story. That day, my 30th birthday, totally changed my life. I woke up in a state of shock, realizing I wasn't a kid anymore. Until I was 29 years and 364 days old, I still felt like a teenager.

I was born knowing one good thing. I knew it was very important to do what I love to do. I had that piece of the puzzle, which is something a lot of people take years to learn. Some people never learn. I was born with that, so I knew it was important to do what I love and to ignore what my parents wanted me to do. My dad wanted me to go into business. I had no interest in that. I became a musician and an actor in my 20s.

I did what I loved, but I had no idea how to be successful doing what I loved. In fact, it was kind of cool to be a starving artist through my 20s, and it was fine until the day I turned 30. When I turned 30, I literally spent most of the day pacing up and down my little slum single room apartment I had in a funky part of Oakland, California. It was $65 a month. This was 30 years ago. So, it was cheap, but even then I was scrounging. It took a lot of time to get my $65 together. I do remember thinking it was almost magical the way I just came up with $65—because I had no money in the bank, and I had no job. I had a rock band before that fell apart. Everything in my 20s, looking back, was like I had the opposite of the Midas touch. Everything fell apart that I got involved with. I got into a theater company right out of college. That fell apart. I got into another company and that totally fell apart. I went to a Zen center and got kicked out for breaking the rules. I finally had a rock band that fell apart. Then I even had little odd jobs that lasted two days as a bus boy and a dishwasher before I was fired for being too slow. I lasted one day doing yard work. They did not ask me to return after a day. So, then I turned 30 and I had no job, no money, nothing. I tried a "back-to-the-land" thing. That was a disaster. I lasted about five months. But, the day that I turned 30, I just paced back and forth and thought about my life in a new way.

I hadn't even really thought about what I wanted to do with my life or the trajectory of my life or anything. I just had been sort of following around other stronger people. I hadn't set a course for myself. I realized it the day I turned 30. I remember pacing up and down, thinking, "Okay, what's the best thing to do? What do I do? How do I begin doing what I need to do?"

> *Everything in my 20s, looking back, was like I had the opposite of the Midas touch. Everything fell apart that I got involved with. I got into a theater company right out of college. That fell apart. I got into another company and that totally fell apart. I went to a Zen center and got kicked out for breaking the rules.*

Then I remembered a game we played when I was 22 and doing that "back-to-the land" experiment. We all sat around the fire one night, and this couple said, "Let's play a game we play at church camp. Let's imagine five years have passed and everything has gone as well as we could imagine. What would your life look like?" We went around the fire, and I don't remember a word of what I said, so it had obviously no impact in my life whatsoever. But I remembered playing that game on my 30th birthday alone in my apartment. This time, a little voice in my head said: this is a good idea. Start here. And I did something that, to this day, I teach. I took a sheet of paper. This time I wrote it down. I put "Ideal Scene" at the top in big letters, and I just imagined five years had passed and everything had gone as well as I could imagine regarding what my life would look like. Much to my amazement, what spilled out was that I had this successful publishing company producing my books and my music and those of other people too, and it cruised along effortlessly and easily, and it left me with plenty of time to write and to have creative time for myself and basically to be lazy. And I had this big white home on the hill in Marin County, CA just north of San Francisco, across the bay from where I was. I had driven through Marin County, and I said, "This is like paradise. It's one of the most beautiful places on earth."

So, that was my dream. And then, as I dared think about it, even though I was already assaulted by thoughts and fears, I added that if I dare to think about my ideal, I want a life of ease. I don't want to work too hard. None of this 40 hour a week bit. That, to me, always felt inhumane. I had the 40 hour a week jobs in my 20s. I did not like them. They didn't leave me enough time for myself and my creativity, so I added, "I want a life of ease. I want success with ease." And then I was assaulted by doubts and fears, and dealing with those doubts and fears became the most important thing I did. So, to this day, I tell people the most important thing to do is set your course. Make those goals. Dare to dream. And then deal with the doubts and fears that come up, but don't let them get you off track for too long. Just keep going back to that dream.

MELISSA: Do you have any recommendations for how to deal with the doubts and fears?

MARC: I do. One thing that helped me was the knowledge that a plane is off course over 95% of the time, but a pilot keeps correcting over and over, and they reach their destination. I remember that when I heard that I thought, that's the story of my life. Once you set a goal, once you dare to dream, you set a course, and whatever you do, you move toward it. It's always just small obvious steps. A journey of a thousand miles begins with one small step, and then just another small step. There's no huge leaps you make. You just take the little obvious steps in front of you when you set your course.

But then all those doubts and fears get us off course, and as long as we just keep correcting we can be off course most of the time and still reach our destination. It's comforting. I remember thinking, in fact, when I wrote a book called A Visionary Life that maybe we had to be on course 51% of the time. But, when I really thought about it, I realized, no, I was off course more than that. I was frustrated. It wasn't working. All these emotional things, all these problems and challenges were in front of me, and I was off course more than I was on course. That's why I love that metaphor of a plane. I think that's true in our lives. We can be off course most of the time, but if we just continue to return to our goal, our dream, our plan and take the next obvious little step, over time we will reach our goal.

MELISSA: In your most recent book, *The Greatest Secret of All*, you reveal that while it's wonderful to know how to create wealth and success, the key to a happy, fulfilled life is really something deeper, which can also be obtained by the same methods. Can you talk about what that something is and how people can attain it?

MARC: Every wealthy person will tell you that wealth does not make you happy. And maybe some people have to obtain a certain level of wealth before they figure that out, but, in fact, the inspiration for the book *The Greatest Secret of All* came after first I saw the movie "The Secret." Eckhart Tolle and I watched it, and afterwards I asked him how he liked it. He said, "It's good, it's good," and I thought yeah, it's okay, and I said, "I wish they would have interviewed you, Eckhart, or someone else who would have added some depth to it and added the fact that yes, you can create this stuff, you can manifest the secret of manifestation." It's very simple. No one is hiding anything. I've already said that you just set a course, make a clear goal. You take the next obvious step in front of you. You let the doubts and fears arise, but then you get back and take the next step.

That's the secret of manifestation. The older I get, the more simply I see it and the more effective it all is. Yes, anybody can learn the secret of manifestation. That's great, but there are far greater things in life. Right after seeing "The Secret," two nights later, I saw a bio on PBS of J. Paul Getty. He was the richest man in the world of his time, and he was one of the most miserable people anyone had ever met. It was pathetic. The story of his life not only made me sad; it gave me this lump in my stomach of real sadness for this pathetic man who didn't understand the things that are far more important than money. All he knew about was money. And he sacrificed his family. He sacrificed everything. He ended up alone and rich. He had four or five different wives. They all ended in divorce. He had five children. He never even held his own sons. He would leave when his wife got pregnant. He would freak out and fly out to another continent and divorce her. The poor man. It was pathetic. And seeing those two things together, "The Secret" and the J. Paul Getty thing, just kept these ideas coming through my mind. I can simply say it: I can simply write that there are far greater secrets than the secret of manifestation, the so-called secret.

It's not a secret. I just told it to you. There are far greater non-secrets to a life well lived. And those are, of course, to love one another, and to love and serve yourself and others. That's the message I get—that the greatest secret of all is always based

> *It's very simple. No one is hiding anything. I've already said that you just set a course, make a clear goal. You take the next obvious step in front of you. You let the doubts and fears arise, but then you get back and take the next step.*

on love and loving first of all ourselves and then all others. That will never take you on any wrong path. That's the greatest secret to a life well lived. It's also very concrete good sense for your business and career. To be guided by that fact that you're there to love and serve other people. If the banks on Wall Street would have remembered that simple fact, they wouldn't have gone bankrupt. They wouldn't have had to collapse because a purpose of the bank is to serve other people's financial needs. They forgot that. They thought the purpose of their careers was to make as much money as possible. That's the worst possible way to operate—trying to just make as much money as possible—because you end up hurting yourself as well as other people. So, it's good solid business guidance to love and serve yourself and others in your career and business.

MELISSA: Do you have any tips for people to help recognize when they're on or off course? There are such subtle ways to get pulled off course.

MARC: It can happen both in our thinking and in our emotions. In our thinking, it can happen when we get overwhelmed with problems and obstacles, or when we get frustrated with details or all the things that can take us off course. In our emotions, of course, any kind of frustration or anxiety can do it. All of that stuff takes us off course.

I've done a new course that will be a book called *A Course in Magic*, and I was looking at the Kabbalah, you know, the stages of creation that the Kabbalah represents. Right in the middle of the Kabbalah is where the creation happens. The middle pillar, they call it. The top one is pure spirit. The next one is focused mind, not going off left and then right, not getting distracted by other possibilities or by this problem or that. Then it goes down to focused emotion—that focused meaning really has the power of love behind it, and it does not get too distracted by frustration or anxiety or doubts and fears. Once you've got a clear, focused thought with the emotion of love behind it, it will manifest. The bottom of the middle pillar is manifestation, and that's the way I see it—when you do train and dare to dream and get focused and don't get too distracted. Some people, a lot of people, including me, get distracted by so many other possibilities. "Oh, I have this idea, but that's a good idea too. I could do this and then of course there's this totally different thing that's back there," and our minds can go in too many creative directions so that we forget to focus on one long enough to bring it into being.

Well, pick one thing at a time. You can do a lot. A lot of successful people do a lot of different things successfully. You can have several things you do and are good at and successful at, but of course you do them one at a time. You focus on one thing and take the next steps that you need to take. Once I set my course, once I got a clear focus, I would start to make plans. Simple one page plans. And always the next step was so obvious. It always felt like, "Gee, why didn't I think of that before," or "that's simple," or "that's just a phone call." The next step became very obvious and clear as I just kept focusing on my goal and affirming that I was creating that goal in an easy and relaxed manner and a healthy and positive way. That affirmation worked for me.

MELISSA: You yourself are someone who is involved in so many activities— music, writing, publishing, and teaching. One thing I observed from studying you and your work is that it seems your success is partly from having a core purpose from which all of the activities stem. Can you talk about what you visualize as your core purpose?

MARC: In some of my seminars I've had people meditate on their purpose and write their purpose and then share it. A good way to get there is to reflect on the word "vocation," which means "calling." Or for some people, the word "mission" is inspiring. "Purpose" scares them, so I have them reflect on their vocation, mission or purpose. Whatever feels right to you—reflect on that and write on that. That's very good. I never really did that until I was well on my way. I found just doing my ideal thing, when I dared dream of my ideal, the ideal life—that the purpose is embedded right in there. Just like every major goal is embedded in that ideal scene.

The purpose was there without even thinking about it. When I dared to dream of the life of my dreams five years in the future, that's what I challenge myself to dare to dream. Then within that, your purpose becomes obvious, so I didn't reflect for quite a while or put into words what my purpose really is. My purpose didn't guide me so much as my ideal scene led me step

> *I challenge everyone to think of this and put it in their own words: What's the most important thing in life? What is the greatest secret of all?*

by step to all my goals. It led me to finally realize the greatest secret of all, in my own words. I challenge everyone to think of this and put it in their own words: What's the most important thing in life? What is the greatest secret of all?

For me, it led to that phrase "love and serve yourself and others." Also, it's wonderful to write your purpose and reflect it, but I think purpose isn't something you share with the world. If you're an entrepreneur or even an artist, a mission statement, instead, is a great thing to share with the world. Our company, New World Library, has a mission statement: We create books and other media that change people's lives in the world. That's a wonderful mission statement to share with the world.

MELISSA: That's exactly what New World Library has done, too. How do you know when you come across something with this incredible power to change people's lives?

MARC: People always ask me what we're looking for, and I typically say, projects we fall in love with, projects that just need to be out there. You have that sense. When we find a project we love, and one of us says, "I learned so much from this. This is so great. I love this stuff," we publish it, and it has that effect on other people. I have always said that whatever I love and what affects my life will affect millions of other people in the same way. When we say, "This is really great stuff but I've heard it before," or "It's not for me, but I think there's a lot that other people might get from it," those things don't do well. Somebody here really has to love it and find it really, really meaningful for themselves, and then it does well and proves meaningful for all kinds of people.

MELISSA: I want to ask you a question about your music before we run out of time. I listened to your CDs, and, for me, it was like embarking on a journey inward at the same time as trekking around the cosmos. How do you achieve this simultaneous intimacy and expansiveness within a single piece?

MARC: Oh, what a wonderful question. I've never been asked anything like that. All I can say about my music is the same thing Eckhart said about his writing. I asked him why he thought The Power of Now did so well. And he just smiled and said, "Well, every sentence came from presence." That's all he said. He waited to write every sentence until presence was there. He even showed me the house in Sausalito where he began to write The Power of Now, and then he went back to England, and he couldn't write in England. And he tried many times. But he never got anything from presence. Then he came back here to the west coast and ended up in Vancouver, and that's where he finished the book. He said there's something about America and maybe the west coast specifically, but that helped him get into presence. And that is why that book is so spectacular and so quotable. Every sentence just came from a quiet place of presence. I know in my music that's the only place it comes from. That's the only place it can come from. When I'm just absolutely quiet, and when I'm not trying to do anything, when I get out of the way, the music happens.

MELISSA: Wow. It's almost like mediation.

MARC: It is. I've found that good music is a wonderful meditation tool, because when we listen to music, we love what happens. We're in a wonderful place.

MELISSA: I've noticed that, as with all great teachers, you offer your guidance in a variety of formats that accommodate different learning styles. You have the blog, podcasts, seminars, audio courses. There's so much out there from you. Do you have recommendations for people for how to choose, according to their own learning style, where the best place is to begin exploring your work?

MARC: Yes, different people definitely learn in different ways. Some are audio learners—just listening to talks is beautiful. And others are more visual. I'm often asked which book to start with and I say, "Well, are you the type of person who can really go through a big course, or are you an entrepreneur, or are you kind of lazy, like I am basically?" If they say they can go through a big course, I say, "The Millionaire Course. Work through that." It's not a great title. It should be called "Success with Ease." It's the only book that says that although being a millionaire is a fine goal, and it's very concrete, it's not important in the least. It's all about defining what success really means for you and then creating it. But if you are too lazy to move through a big book like that, then my little Type-Z Guide is for lazy people. The Greatest Secret of All is summarized very

> *It's the only book that says that although being a millionaire is a fine goal, and it's very concrete, it's not important in the least. It's all about defining what success really means for you and then creating it.*

simply in very few pages. I promised I would try to give the essence away of what I know every time I talked and every time I wrote. So, the essence is in everything.

MELISSA: You've created an interesting style in *The Greatest Secret of All*—how in addition to the full text, you have the key points set off so that really people can read the book in two different ways. If they want to they can go deeply, or they can just glean the main points. When did it become apparent to you that this would be a good style to communicate the message?

MARC: I've been doing that for years. I remember when I first saw a business plan when I started the company. It had all the text on right hand pages, and then the left hand pages just had one sentence each that summarized everything. I was struck by that format and realized, this is to be read by busy people because a great many of them will just read that one sentence. I thought, that's a good writing style because it forces you as a writer to really say it briefly. You really cut through all the words and break down on that one page in one sentence what you want to retain and remember.

MELISSA: We're about to run out of time. Do you have any future courses, works, or publications you'd like to announce?

MARC: Oh, thanks for that. I do have free seminars on the first Wednesday of every month. My other things aren't scheduled yet, but just go to www.marcallen.com. It has upcoming events and links to my music, books and blogs.

Photograph by Eric Antoniou

ROBERT PINSKY

JUNE 20, 2011

MELISSA: Our interview this evening is with Robert Pinsky. Pinsky is a poet who has served three terms as United States Poet Laureate, and he is also an acclaimed literary critic and the best-selling translator of *The Inferno of Dante.* He has received numerous awards for his poetry and translations, including the Lenore Marshall Award, the Ambassador Book Award of the English Speaking Union, the PEN/Voelcker Award, the William Carlos Williams Prize, and the Theodore M. Roethke Memorial Poetry Award. He currently teaches in the graduate writing program at Boston University and serves as the poetry editor for *Slate.* His most recent collection of poetry is Selected Poems. Lloyd Schwarz, of *The Boston Phoenix,* has said of Pinsky, "In his poems, Pinsky talks with democratic warmth and intimacy, to the common things of this world. His extraordinary poems remind us that he has always embodied the very ideal he proposes for what a poet can do."

Hi. How are you doing tonight?

ROBERT: Very well, thank you, Melissa. Glad to be talking to you.

MELISSA: I'm so happy to be talking to you as well. I'm going to jump in with a couple of big questions, and then, from there, we can get more specific and hear some poems.

ROBERT: I will try to give some medium-sized answers.

MELISSA: Wonderful! So, in your lecture, "Modernism and Memory," you said that to "'be born for death' is to need to create memory that is larger than one generation," and you also said that the treasure of memory can only be properly cared for if it's transformed. I know you're a big fan of Walt Whitman and William Carlos Williams. Can you talk about the particular ways in which your own poetry might be considered a transformation of the poetic treasures of Whitman and Williams?

ROBERT: The "born for death" phrase is from John Keats's great poem, "Ode to a Nightingale." He says the bird sings the same song its grandparents and great-grandparents sang: "thou wast not born for death, immortal bird."

At some point, it occurred to me that in choosing ancestors like Whitman and Williams, as well as my literal ancestors—the various

Pinskys and Eisenbergs that stretch back behind me—I am choosing to understand that I was born for death, as were Whitman and Williams and Keats and David Pinsky and Morris Eisenberg and Becky Eisenberg and Rose Schecter.

We are all born for death, and we remember certain things. I remember very well my grandmother Rose's tombstone and her picture in Long Branch, NJ. She died as a young woman in childbirth, decades before I was

I'm very aware that it's my job to choose, from all those ancestors, the literal and figurative progenitors—many of them are both— to choose what I pass on to my literal and figurative descendants.

born. And I remember my grandfather, Dave Pinsky, coming by our apartment one day and telling my mother I would not be going to school that day. I was in about the third or fourth grade. He would take me in to New York for lunch. I met Jack Dempsey there, at his restaurant, where my Grandfather Dave and I ate.

In a similar way, I remember "look for me under your boot soles"(*Song of Myself*, Walt Whitman) and "a copper of an 8 strip beaten lengthwise at right angles and lies ready to edge the coping," (*Fine Work with Pitch and Copper*, William Carlos Williams), and I'm very aware that it's my job to choose, from all those ancestors, the literal and figurative progenitors—many of them are both—to choose what I pass on to my literal and figurative descendants.

And I must say, I have more intense feelings about that than I do about ideas of worship and God. I guess I'm like an ancient pagan. I think a lot about ancestors and descendants.

MELISSA: I love that. It reminds me of another thing you said in that same lecture: "We don't worship our ancestors. We consult them."

ROBERT: Yes, when I was in Africa, on the way to see the sangoma, who goes into a trance and gets words from the ancestors, my guide told me, "Remember: we Zulu do not worship our ancestors. We consult them." When I heard that, I felt I had discovered my own belief. I'm sort of paraphrasing my poem "Creole" . . . which you can hear on iTunes, where I say it with music by the wonderful pianist Laurence Hobgood.

MELISSA: It's great how you applied that to poetry.

You've said many times, most recently in the PBS News Hour, that poetry is too fundamental and too large to need an advocate, and I believe that is true.

Yet, looking at poetry from the perspective that we were just speaking from—as a treasure to be cared for— we do continue to care for it, and I must say no one has done a better job of caring for that treasure than you. So, following your excellent lead, what are some of the things contemporary Americans, and particularly contemporary American poets, can do to also properly care for that treasure?

ROBERT: I believe much more in teachers from kindergarten all the way through graduate school, and in librarians, than I do in marketing moves by organizations and foundations. A lot of official, organized attempts are dumb, I think because they are attempts at marketing rather than caretaking. On the web you can find silly stuff like how to make an Emily Dickinson or Walt Whitman Halloween costume. Or they'll have contests for kids to perform poems dramatically. Or special apps that make the letters of a poem dance around on your cell phone screen. I don't have much sympathy with that kind of elaborate, well-meaning, expensive stuff.

Caretaking, in my view, is simpler and more effective. For example: encourage good teachers and public librarians who do a good job with poetry. Support "Poets in the Schools." For me, that'd be better than the apps and Halloween costumes and declamation contests and promotions.

If you have children, or know someone with children, have the kids sit on the parent's lap and let them listen to Walter de la Mare or Egbert Leer or Robert Louis Stevenson or Dr. Seuss. Read aloud to your children. Read aloud to one another. The Favorite Poem Project– the videos at favoritepoem.org, the Summer Institute for K-12 Educators—is basically a version of that simple idea. In the videos, you see the construction worker reading Whitman, the Cambodian-American immigrant young woman reading an Eliza Yost poem.

Reading the poem aloud is central, and the idea is simple, or let's say it's plain. What's a better feeling than discovering that by reading a poem aloud to yourself a few times you have begun to get it by heart without trying?

MELISSA: One thing I've noticed is that some poets have a tendency to write mostly for other poets. Do you have any advice on how poets can bring their poetry more to the world instead of primarily to each other?

ROBERT: I think it's like being a musician or a dancer or an architect or a painter. You try to make something that would knock you out if you were the audience. So, I

What's a better feeling than discovering that by reading a poem aloud to yourself a few times you have begun to get it by heart without trying?

don't think if I imagined myself being an architect I would want to base it on market surveys. I would try to think about spaces and buildings that give me a good feeling. What kinds of spaces make me feel full of delicious energy, or wonderful calm? Or if you are a musician, you try to play things that just knock you out. If you hadn't made it, you would like to hear it. So, maybe I differ from you in this, Melissa. I don't think about writing for an audience. I think: What if Robert hadn't written this, if he found it in a book or a magazine, would he yawn, or would he stop and say to himself, "I wonder what's on TV," or would he read it?

MELISSA: Your audience is yourself.

ROBERT: Yes and no: it's a matter of imagining myself if I hadn't made the work. You're always, in just about any pursuit—certainly in all the arts—trying to get to that sweet place between liking your work too much, in which case you don't make it any better, and not liking it enough, which makes you want to quit. I think our own joy—the joy I find in Hart Crane, Emily Dickinson, Ben Johnson, or Allen Ginsberg—whatever pleases me in poetry, that's my compass; that's my guide. I guess in a way part of my mind may be imagining Crane or Dickinson reading a line or a phrase, as I compose it. But ultimately, it's one's own internal compass or scales. I can't go by what I think might please Melissa Studdard or might please my friend or what my dad would like to read or what might charm an audience at a poetry reading. It's more like trying to think: What is the kind of thing I adore? How can I make something that is out of my heart the way "Howl" comes from Allen Ginsberg's heart or how "Ode to a Nightingale" comes from John Keats's heart?

The assumption is: I'm not so totally weird that if I would like something, no other person in the world would. And having said that about my own degree of weirdness, I do think: Hmmmm. . . .

MELISSA: You're right. If you worry too much about all those other people and things, you will go crazy with it. I mean for me, it would just cause paralysis, and I wouldn't be able to write.

ROBERT: If you worry about audience in a certain way, you approach your work in an art differently from what I mean. You are a craftsman of a different kind: you want to be popular. And I won't sneer at it. There are people who do market research, and then they design the car. I assume other people try to make a car that appeals to their sense of what a car is or should be. The difference can apply to almost any realm. Among the comic strips in The Boston Globe, there are some strips that I feel are entirely, transparently interested in what a lot of people want. I'm not crazy about them. In contrast, I read Bill Griffith's strip *Zippy the Pinhead*, which I adore, and I feel he is trying to make things that, in the drawing, in the dialogue, and in the continuity, have the kind of joy and playfulness and wackiness and seriousness that he enjoys. I recognize someone who is making art out of the spirit of art. It's not to sneer at the spirit of commerce. Commerce has a place too, but I'm more like Bill Griffith, I hope.

MELISSA: What did you notice about your own poetic evolution when you were compiling *Selected Poems*? Did you learn anything significant about who you've been as a poet or where you would like to go next?

ROBERT: You always want to do something different, and I was relieved to find, as I went through the poems, that I did feel as if each book seemed to take a new direction. I asked myself, "What haven't you been able to do yet?" And the answer was: "To make different kinds of lines." I know that some of my young students wonder why I still use the capital letter at the beginning of a line, and I have both the stupid and the smart answer to that question.

The stupid answer is: Almost everybody nowadays uses the lower case at the beginning of the line, so why not be different?

A slightly smarter answer is: I think more than many people, I am really very aware of lines. The sound of lines, of each line. I've never written a sonnet or villanelle or sestina. I'm not interested in "forms," in that sense; but I am very interested in *form* as it works in different kinds of lines. As a reader, I come across one book with a lot of long lines, or another one with a lot of short lines and I try to hear the lines and the sentences, how they work together. Possibly I notice that the lines sound kind of close to pentameters or rather far off—sometimes regardless of the typography. I will recognize different ancestors, as in a Blake or a Dickinson moment, or more of a Whitman or Williams moment. And as a writer I hope the poems I'm writing right now are doing something new for me, something different than anything in my *Selected Poems*.

MELISSA: *Selected Poems* has had a beautiful critical reception. I'm thinking, in particular, of a review by David Kaufmann, entitled "Expansive," from *The Tablet*. One thing that struck him about the collection is the way it's structured differently than most selected works. Could you tell us a bit about how and why you structured it the way you did?

ROBERT: One sort of practical, or audience-concerned factor came into the reverse chronology—starting with the most recent books and ending with *An Explanation of America* and then *Sadness And Happiness*: those early books contain some quite long poems. Thinking about readers new to my work, in particular quite young ones, say a teenager, I thought that more clearly lyrical or song-like poems might make a better beginning. So, my *Selected* can begin with "Rhyme."

MELISSA: I'd love to hear you read a poem from *Selected Poems*. Would you read "Gulf Music?"

ROBERT: I will be happy to read "Gulf Music." It might be good to warn your readers that I quote two things in the poem. I quote the great piano player and vocalist, Professor Longhair, at the beginning, and I also quote a Hebrew song from the Haggadah, the narrative Passover service. I not only quote the two, Longhair and Haggadah—they get mixed up together.

Gulf Music

Mallah walla tella bella. Trah mah trah-la, la-la-la,
Mah la belle. Ippa Fano wanna bella, wella-wah.

The hurricane of September 8, 1900 devastated
Galveston, Texas. Some 8,000 people died.

The Pearl City almost obliterated. Still the worst natural
Calamity in American history, Woh mallah-walla.

Eight years later Morris Eisenberg sailing from Lübeck
Entered the States through the still-wounded port of Galveston.

1908, eeloo hotesy, hotesy-ahnoo, hotesy ahnoo mi-Mizraim
Or you could say "Morris" was his name. A Moshe.

Ippa Fano wanna bella woh. The New Orleans musician called
Professor Longhair was named Henry Roeland Byrd.

Not heroic not nostalgic not learnëd. Made-up names:
Hum a few bars and we'll homme-la-la. Woh ohma-dallah.

Longhair or Henry and his wife Alice joined the Civil Defense
Special Forces 714. Alice was a Colonel, he a Lieutenant.

Here they are in uniforms and caps, pistols in holsters.
Hotesy anno, Ippa Fano trah ma dollah, tra la la.

Morris took the name "Eisenberg" after the rich man from
His shtetl who in 1908 owned a town in Arkansas.

Most of this is made up, but the immigration papers did
Require him to renounce all loyalty to Czar Nicholas.

As he signed to that, he must have thought to himself
The Yiddish equivalent of *No Problem*, Mah la belle.

Hotesy hotesy-ahno. Wella-mallah widda dallah,
Mah fanna-well. A townful of people named Eisenberg.

The past is not decent or orderly, it is made-up and devious.
The man was correct when he said it's not even past.

Look up at the waters from the causeway where you stand:
Lime causeway made of grunts and halfway-forgettings

On a foundation of crushed oyster shells. Roadbed
Paved with abandonments, shored up by haunts.

Becky was a teenager married to an older man. After she
Met Morris, in 1910 or so, she swapped Eisenbergs.

They rode out of Arkansas on his motorcycle, well-ah-way.
Wed-away. "Mizraim" is Egypt, I remember that much.

The storm bulldozed Galveston with a great rake of debris.
In the September heat the smell of the dead was unbearable.

Hotesy hotesy ahnoo. "Professor" the New Orleans title
For any piano player. He had a Caribbean left hand,

A boogie-woogie right. Civil Defense Special Forces 714
Organized for disasters, mainly hurricanes. Floods.

New Orleans style borrowing this and that, ah wail-ah-way la-la,
They probably got "714" from Joe Friday's badge number

On *Dragnet.* Jack Webb chose the number in memory
Of Babe Ruth's 714 home runs, the old record.

As living memory of the great hurricanes of the thirties
And the fifties dissolved, Civil Defense Forces 714

Also dissolved, washed away for well or ill – yet nothing
Ever entirely abandoned through generations forget, and ah

Well the partial forgetting embellishes everything all the more:
Alla-mallah, mi-Mizraim, try my tra-la, hotesy-totesy.

Dollars, dolors. Callings and contrivances. King Zulu. Comus.
Sephardic ju-ju and verses. Voodoo mojo, Special Forces.

Henry formed a group named Professor Longhair and his
Shuffling Hungarians. After so much renunciation

And invention, is this the image of the promised end?
All music haunted by all the music of dead forever.

Becky haunted forever by Pearl the daughter she abandoned
For love, O try my tra-la-la, ma la belle, mah walla-woe.

MELISSA: Thank you. That was fantastic. I think you just proved that you can do call and response with yourself, right?

ROBERT: I guess so—thanks! Refrain is quite basic to poetry. It's in all the ballads. It's in song. And I like doing something very traditional in a somewhat crazy, weird, different way. The poem is so much about what you and I were just discussing, in relation to the past. In New Orleans, you know—it is "Gulf Music"—during Katrina, the Special Forces 714 I mention in the poem had dissolved, but people in New Orleans started that the Special

Forces as a civic organization in the '30s explicitly to deal with natural disasters, hurricanes. They organized this structure, this traditional organization, to preserve order and help people in times of floods and hurricanes. In that case, the ancestral tradition didn't endure quite long enough. TV came in. There were too many years since a really big hurricane, and when they really needed it, it wasn't quite there anymore. To me, that's one of the risks and sadnesses of all of the glories of civilization––that we establish traditions to take care of the world and of the people, and sometimes they suffice, and sometimes they wither.

> *To me, that's one of the risks and sadnesses of all of the glories of civilization—that we establish traditions to take care of the world and of the people, and sometimes they suffice, and sometimes they wither.*

MELISSA: It's interesting—I remember you said somewhere that all of your poems are about the same thing—the fact that there is history in everything. Why did you choose that particular theme? Or did it choose you?

ROBERT: The latter, I think. Who knows why you think about a certain thing, but it's possible to speculate. I grew up in a historic town, Long Branch, New Jersey. It had been the capital of many presidents. Grant went there in the summer. Garfield loved it. Garfield died in Long Branch after he was shot. It was what used to be, as the sign said when you entered the town, "America's First Seashore Resort," so there's that background. And then I was also fascinated by the history of my parents and grandparents who came to the town in the 20th century. My grandfather, Dave Pinsky, had a bar when I knew him, but in the twenties he had been a bootlegger, and that had a certain fascination for me. I don't know why the past means so much to me. I had a nominally orthodox Jewish upbringing, and it was so nominal that I promised myself I wouldn't have to do it anymore.

MELISSA: Speaking of leaving things behind, I've noticed that memory is just as important as history to your poems, and you've been writing a lot lately about forgetting. Can you talk about the significance of that as well?

ROBERT: Forgetting is a form of memory: the forgetting of Babe Ruth's 714 home runs; the forgetting of Joe Friday's badge number, 714; the forgetting of Special Forces 714 in New Orleans. All those instances of forgetting are part of the story (or stories?) I try to remember in "Gulf Music," like the forgetting of my grandfather Eisenberg's first surname, when he took the surname Eisenberg—because in that little Arkansas shtetl, they are all called Eisenberg, including the man who took his wife away from him. And I can't conceive remembering without forgetting. Neither term would have any meaning without the other. So, if you are going to write about remembering, you certainly are obliged to write about forgetting as well.

MELISSA: Going back to your wonderful poem, "Gulf Music"—I love the scatting, and I noticed the call and response, and I know you have a strong musical background, so I'm wondering what other ways you see your musical background manifesting in your poetry.

ROBERT: I've always liked refrains. I've always liked "nonsense" and as a reader I enjoy Shakespeare's "heigh-ho"s and "hey-nonny-

nonny"s— for him and his friends an equivalent of pop music's "yeah-yeah" or "baby, baby." But "nonsense" can be a deceptive term. To somebody who doesn't know Hebrew, "Hotesy hotesy ahnoo" sounds like nonsense. Professor Longhair's "tella mallah tella donna ma la belle" may sound like nonsense, I suppose, if you don't speak any English or French or Creole, or if you are numb to certain kinds of implication. Sense is a matter of degree, I think. The grunts, the sounds of words, the physical component of language: again, my sense of all that goes back to my childhood. The one distinctly beautiful thing in those long services I endured on Saturday mornings was cantorial singing. I learned Hebrew phonetically. I couldn't understand 80% of what was being sung, though I sort of had the general idea. And the singing by the cantor was beautiful.

You're right—in my high school days and early college years, I was still trying to be a musician, though gradually I realized I was going to be better off trying to make poems than trying to be a musician, though as I think you know, lately, I have been performing rather a lot with musicians.

MELISSA: Yes, I would love to hear more about your performances with musicians.

ROBERT: I've been fortunate to perform with many great musicians, including Ben Allison, Bobby Bradford, Andrew Cyrille, Vijay Iyer, Rakalam Bob Moses, Stan Strickland. I wrote a piece for Slate on the subject, with some video/audio clips: it is at http://tinyurl.com/6rqh9y4. I think the approach these musicians and I take is unique, unlike other ways of combining words and music. I am a non-singing vocalist, trying to use the melodies and cadences of a poem as a musical element. It is more like rap than it is like an art song or an actor with background music. But instead of rap rhythms or idiom, the rhythms and idiom of . . . well, of my poems, that voice. The verb the musicians and I use is "playing." We play music together. The CD from Circumstantial Productions, POEMJAZZ, exemplifies what I mean—much better than an explanation.

That has been a great outcome: performing (and recording) with the superlative pianist Laurence Hobgood. The CD is Laurence and me, the result of two more or less all-day studio sessions. From his work with Kurt Elling, Laurence has developed a great sensitivity to words, along with his superb, pure chops as a jazz musician, his gifted work as arranger for Kurt. Laurence reads the poems very attentively, and plays with a copy of the text in front of him.

MELISSA: Robert, I'm a huge fan of your poetry, and I must say that these musical collaborations are as deeply compelling as are the poems themselves. I could listen to them all day, every day!

I would love to know more about your composition process. I know it isn't really the same for all poems, but maybe, just taking this particular poem, "Gulf Music," can you talk about what it was like for you? Were you led by the sounds?

> *I am a non-singing vocalist, trying to use the melodies and cadences of a poem as a musical element.*

ROBERT: I knew I wanted to start the poem with that call, with pure phonetic. "Mah la belle, my beautiful"—it has meaning. As I just said, it's a matter of degree. You can't have pure nonsense anymore than you can have pure meaning. There's always some grunt;

there's always some significance. I knew I wanted to start that way, and I knew I wanted to make these separate, self-contained couplets. I wanted to have each unit of form about the same length, and I wanted the poem to move around rapidly, even aggressively. A settled symmetry and an unsettling variety, both.

And exactly what was going to come into it in the way of history, I wasn't sure. I knew it had to have New Orleans in it, and Professor Longhair. The germinating fact was that he and his wife belonged to an institution (Special Forces 714) that foundered and faded too soon for when it was needed, the stress and destruction of Hurricane Katrina.

That the classic TV detective Joe Friday was going to come into it was a surprise. I knew that the Passover hymn, or song, was going to come in. That Pearl, the lost, abandoned half-sister of my mother, Pearl abandoned after her mother changed one Eisenberg man for another—I didn't know Pearl was going to come into it. I almost thought she couldn't because Galveston, Texas's nickname has been the Pearl City: a coincidence that seemed maybe too large. But I knew that the South was going to be important. My mother was born in Arkansas. My grandfather did enter the country as part of what historians call the Houston Project, and his father and uncle moved to Mississippi. A certain number of Eastern, Ashkenazi Jews came into the south through the Port of Galveston, through that project supported by wealthy, long-settled German Jews in New York.

Certainly I knew the poem was going to have history in it, Melissa. Exactly what history and how it was going to come in I had to discover, but I knew some would be personal, some more impersonal, and that they would blend; I just sort of felt through as I went through the poem. But I had the unaffected tune in the couplets. I had a kind of tune or a harmonic structure in the couplets, and then I had to listen, to determine how I was going to weave "Mallah walla tella bella" and "hotesy, hotesy-ahnoo" : weave them in, and at a crucial moment near the end weave them together.

I mean the passage, "King Zulu. Comus. /Sephardic ju-ju and verses. Voodoo mojo, Special Forces." Reading "Gulf Music," I still sometimes can't keep from laughing to myself every time I read the name of Henry Roeland Byrd's group: "Pro-

> *If you're having a good time, you don't need to understand every single thing. You can have fun, or feel deeply moved, at the opera, or listening to rap music, or listening to anything, without necessarily understanding everything in it.*

fessor Longhair and his Shuffling Hungarians." It is a very witty name, a wonderful composition in itself. And it's all about this cultural syncretism, the mish-mash of putting a lot of things together, an action. I love in American culture: our national capacity for outrageous, mongrel invention. And it shows that Henry Roeland Bird, known as "Professor Longhair," was well aware of that quality of mongrel invention, very much in control of it in his art, and rather sophisticated about it. He had to laugh at that band name, and I smile every time I arrive at it.

MELISSA: The poem and the mish-mashing you're talking about are so energetic, so exciting. I love what you said before, not in this interview, but in another one I've heard—that you don't really have to understand what's in a poem, and that's what's wonderful about poetry—that it is what it is, to some extent, and the parts we don't understand are carried by context.

ROBERT: If you're having a good time, you don't need to understand every single thing. You can have fun, or feel deeply moved, at the opera, or listening to rap music, or listening to anything, without necessarily understanding everything in it.

MELISSA: Right.

ROBERT: And if the audience is not having a good time, clarity is no use. It doesn't help.

MELISSA: That's right. The more people understand that, the less likely it is that those who are intimidated by poetry will continue to feel intimidated.

ROBERT: I think a lot of well-meaning teaching and literary criticism has given people the idea that the poem is, first of all, an occasion for the reader to say smart things about the poem. Smart things are good, understanding is desirable, the more the better—but they come in due course. The first thing, the primary thing, is to enjoy the way it sounds.

MELISSA: That's a great point. I can't believe we're out of time already. It's been a real delight speaking with you. Thank you so much.

ROBERT: My pleasure, Melissa. Thank you.

Photograph by Maria Elena Boekemeyer

LOIS P. JONES

JULY 24, 2011

MELISSA: Our interview this evening is with Lois P. Jones. Jones's poetry and photographs have been published widely in print and on-line journals in the U.S. and abroad. She is co-founder of Word Walker Press and since 2008 has hosted KPFK's Poets Café in Los Angeles (90.7 FM Pacifica Radio), which airs on the 2nd, 4th and 5th Wednesdays at 8:30 p.m. Lois co-produces Moonday in the Village, a west side reading, and is co-host of Moonday's east side poetry reading at Flintridge Books. She is the Poetry Editor of *Kyoto Journal* and a recent Pushcart Nominee as well as a nominee for Best New Poets. Lois is also a frequent participant in the yearly San Miguel Poetry Week. In 2010, her poem "Ouija" was featured by IBPC as Poem of the Year.

Welcome, Lois. It's so wonderful to have you on the show.

LOIS: Thank you. It's such a great honor to be here and just lovely to chat with you, Melissa. I've been a fan of *Tiferet* for several years. I love what Donna is doing, and I was introduced to a number of great poets through Tiferet, including J.P. Dancing Bear and others. I've had the honor of having poems and a photograph or two in *Tiferet*, and I feel deeply connected to the spiritual aspect of the journal—that being a major part of my life and influence.

MELISSA: I feel the same way. Donna is doing amazing things with the journal.

So, in an interview with the *Tacoma Weekly* you said, "I believe that inspiration is not just a momentary urge but a way of being. It is an openness to the world around you." What I'd like to know is how you achieve this openness and sustain it.

LOIS: That's a great question. It has a lot to do with being very involved in what's going on around you. I belong to a number of poetry groups. One of them is Poets on Site, which is run by Kath Abela Wilson and we are active in going to museums, going out in nature and to exhibits where we are actually interacting with the environment and using that as a jumping off point to write poetry.

So, that's more along the practical side of inspiration. With the different involvements I have, it seems that poetry is happening pretty much 24/7, whether with Poets on Site or because I'm moderating an internet board and connected that way.

Reading the work of others is also a great source of, not only inspiration, but, a way of evolving as a poet—being able to reach into what past and contemporary poets have to say and then seeing

> *The kind of poetry I like to write and read is poetry of transcendence, so I begin with the physical as a jumping off point, and it seems to lead to the metaphysical and spiritual.*

where that leads you in your own writing and your own thought process.

The third part of this answer is more or less a personal, spiritual one. You are tuned into your own particular path, whatever that might be. That leads you to a higher awareness and that awareness, if you are connecting it with some creative aspect of life, can only lead you to inspiration.

MELISSA: Speaking of going to the museum and out into nature for inspiration, one of the things that strikes me about your poetry is the blending of art, humanity, and the natural world. When you look at art or nature in your poems, there's never a lens or separation from humanity. Art and nature are humanity—even in the literal sense that a neck is also a painting of a neck, a dune, and a cliffside.

LOIS: Hey! You're taking away my lines.

MELISSA: Let's read it then, and we can talk about it some more.

LOIS: Okay, great. So, this is called "Ways to Paint a Woman," and I was graced and surprised by a painting that a friend of mine from Dubai rendered of me. A portrait of my face. This was about a year ago, and I had no idea it was coming. His name is Ali Al Ameri and I was so moved by this beautiful painting that I decided to write a poem in response.

Ways to Paint a Woman

Sometimes you cannot say
what is in the heart.

Sometimes you have to paint it yellow—
listen with the eyes: honeycomb and maize,

golden rainflowers.
Transform with your softest brush

the way Lorca's bathing girl liquefies
into water–half a head in fire,

sun burning a trail from forehead to cheek.
Graze the mouth with mango. Make time to blend

and take away. Use the green of a blind man
when he says *you're beautiful*

and means *you're timeless.*
Show what the light gave her

washing warmth into a neck
until it's dune, a cliffside

that holds a head of surf.
Paint as you would before you awaken,

when sunlight falls like milkweed
and you are an empty silo

letting her grain fill you—
buttery malt and biscuit

for the love of honey.

MELISSA: Thank you. That was beautiful. Now, we can talk about it. What I see in your poems over and over—I don't want to call it a transformation—is more like a connector. Do you feel like that connection comes into play through the act of writing poetry, or is it in place already for you?

LOIS: The kind of poetry I like to write and read is poetry of transcendence, so I begin with the physical as a jumping off point, and it seems to lead to the metaphysical and spiritual. It's a constant in my writing, and when I look at the ecstatic joy of creation, that's where I want to go in poetry.

Everyone has their own enjoyment of poetry, their own particular genres. We have humorous poetry, and we have poems that are beautiful narratives like the ones by Robert Joseph Stroud, who writes on nature. He also has transcendence too but a lot of his poetry is experiential. For me poetry doesn't have to have experience. It's more of the moment and where that moment leads me to, and, so, in that way, I'm somewhat different in that I don't write typically narrative work.

MELISSA: I know you were strongly influenced by the Latin American poets, and I would say that definitely has a lot to do with your style, which is just lovely. Who are some of the ones who really influenced you?

LOIS: Well, Lorca has come up a number of times. He was one of the first poets I began reading. I fell in love with Poet in New York and several other books. One of his main books, *In Search of Duende*, has what Bly talks about in the book *Leaping Poetry*—you are making this unexpected leap of an image, creating things that resonate with you unexpectedly.

That's what I love most about Lorca. He is has his own particular voice and images. They're startling and sometimes dark and deeply pas-

> *...anyone who wants to create needs to have a certain concept of composition, whether its visual or written.*

sionate. Those were my origins—Lorca, a French poet named Paul Eluard, and then the German-Austrian poet Rainer Maria Rilke, who is probably more the long-distance runner for me as far as influence. And let me also add Pablo Neruda and Eugenio Montejo—and no list would be complete without Jorge Luis Borges.

MELISSA: Let's talk about your photography. I have some pretty good ideas about how your photography has impacted your poetry, but I'd like to know what your experience of it has been and also how you feel your poetry has impacted your photography.

LOIS: I'm just an amateur photographer, but anyone who wants to create needs to have a certain concept of composition, whether it's visual or written, and I think photography allows you to see what the important points need to be and what to get rid of.

This is also the essence of good poetry writing and editing. So, there's a definite relationship there. Sometimes I take photographs that I'm inspired by and write poems to them, but more often I have several other friends who dazzle me with their photography. Peter Shefler is a friend of mine. Another is Leslie Morley, who lives in England. Their photographs move beyond the physical world.

Again, it's a transcendence from the literal graphic image to something way beyond. And that is a talent. I haven't reached that.

MELISSA: I'd have to disagree with you on that.

LOIS: Thank you.

MELISSA: The one I took from your Facebook page and posted on my blog—the one with the benches—is a beautiful study of light and shadows.

LOIS: That makes me think of an additional perspective, which is that a good image is also like a good poem in that it's something the viewer can contribute to. So, you take it away from this two-dimensional world into something that goes off into other dimensions and allows that person to be part of an exchange with art. Really, that's the essence of it.

MELISSA: Interesting. When I was talking about the shadows in that photograph, it made me think about how important shadows and light are to your poetry, as well. Do you think that's the result of your work with photography?

LOIS: I don't think so. I wouldn't say that it really has had an influence. I think they are right now coexisting in an interesting way, but they are not influencing one another. The shadows of one haven't really manifested in the other quite yet.

MELISSA: Do you want to read another poem? Would you like to read "Ouija"?

LOIS: Sure. This one is about a Ouija board, which we know is a device used to contact people who are ghosts or spirits who have moved beyond, and it has a rather dark aspect to it. But I wouldn't say I was trying to connect with the occult in this poem so much as reaching out to a spirit and thinking: What would that person want to say if he could say something now? So, this begins with an epigraph from Lorca and goes like this....

Ouija

*Green sunflowers trembled in the highlands of dusk and the
whole cemetery
began to complain with cardboard mouths and dry rags. —
Federico Garcia Lorca*

You asked for an R, for the ripening of olives
in your garden, the red-tailed hawk

angling over the road, the path
that took you down and away

from the empty room of the body.
The R of reasons, of the ringing that breaks

in a yellow bell tower—the only sound
after the round of shots that shattered

an afternoon. And the T can only be more time,
time to be the clock or the weather vane,

the twilight through your windows
on the page, your pen once again plow

and the places you took me
where I abandoned faith.

A is alone, how you never wanted it,
preferring the company of bishop's

weed and drowsy horses—the warm trace
of the lily and a flame

for the night with its black mouth
that sings your *saeta.*

G is the ghost bird that hovered
at Fuente Grande that you did not wish

to come, for the grave some say you dug
with your own hands,

empty as a mouth full of snow,
as a sky that held no moon that night

only its pure shape to stow
all the names of the dead.

Interestingly about Lorca—he was killed by the Nationalist Militia under the Franco regime, and they're still trying to find where he was buried, because he was buried in a mass grave. So, there are a lot of stories floating around about the incident.

MELISSA: You have another poem specifically about that, don't you?

LOIS: Yes, I do. "Unmarked Grave."

MELISSA: That's it. That's a beautiful poem as well.

LOIS: Thank you.

MELISSA: When you read the poem, I noticed the focus on emptiness, and I've noticed that in a lot of your other poems too, particularly in relation to the artist or creativity—the empty silo, the empty room of the body, and branches. Is this concept of emptiness important to you as a poet? Do you think it's important for the artist in general?

LOIS: Emptiness embodies a place to allow things to come in and not be afraid of silence. In our society we're so inundated with stimulus that to be able to be empty is a joy. It's a beauty. It's something artists have been trying to do for centuries so that they can tap into their own voices.

I love the experience of being with my friends and family, but to be empty is also to be receptive. This actually

> *Emptiness embodies a place to allow things to come in and not be afraid of silence. In our society we're so inundated with stimulus that to be able to be empty is a joy.*

reminds me: I may be jumping ahead, but as an interviewer I've had the good fortune of being supported by a producer, Marlena Bond, who is a genius as far as putting the shows together and allowing this type of freedom where I don't feel that I have to fill up every second. I can allow for the poet who is on the air to have his own space and pace, and that makes for a kind of organic interview experience. So, that was on my mind at that moment.

MELISSA: I'm glad you brought that up because it would be kind of silly for two interviewers to talk and not talk about interviewing. I'm curious about how interviewing has impacted you as a person and also how it has impacted your poetry, because I know your program, Poets Café, is focused specifically on poetry. I know you go very, very deep with it, and it seems that talking to people about poetry at that level would have some kind of wonderful impact for you with your own writing.

LOIS: I want to mention the names of the other hosts because I would be remiss otherwise: Myrenna Ogbu and Jaimes Palacio. But, to answer your question, it's such a huge world because every experience is different, and every poet is different, so I try to connect with the poet's particular aesthetic and life on a very intimate level. That kind of thing does change you. It changes you, it influences you, it allows you inside in a different way than picking up someone's book and reading them, because you are shaping something, you know. I don't know how you feel about this, but it seems for me like every interview is sort of a sculpture, and you are shaping it. You don't know exactly what the final form will be.

MELISSA: Right, you don't know what will happen.

LOIS: No, you don't know. That's the joy of it. You have this fluidity. You have this living thing, and sometimes it transcends into art, when you have those moments. You know, when a poet is reading to you, when he's reading something very close to his or her heart, and it becomes this intense sharing over the airwaves. At the end of the day, for me, it's always about how that person feels. Of course, I want other people to enjoy the show, but I want the poet to feel honored.

MELISSA: I couldn't agree more.

LOIS: I'm looking forward to interviewing you and turning the tables around.

MELISSA: (Laughs) Not now. We're talking about you. So, I want to ask you something that I'm sure should have come up earlier, and it may be too personal—if it is just tell me, and we'll move on—but I'm curious about your spirituality because you've mentioned it a couple of times. In your poetry you don't really name it or focus on it, but it's always there as an undercurrent, and the poems, though not directly about spiritual subject matter, are spiritual themselves. I'm just curious about what's behind it. How do you define your spirituality, or what is your interest in spiritual matters?

LOIS: Spirituality has always been a part of my life. I grew up in the Jewish faith, and I'm still connected with it culturally, although not as much from a dogmatic perspective. I appreciate its focus and emphasis, and I have had a lot of experiences which I should probably write about one day, but they were more ritual than spiritual as I was growing up.

And going to synagogue and observing traditions and seeing my grandmother in the crowd, all of us praying—these are influences from my past, but I always had this very strong urge to head towards a Gnostic sensibility, and so it's been a long road toward finding something for me that actually satisfied a lot of questions I had and gave me my own sense of, not only relief from the past, but a perspective on the joy of life, the depth of humanity, and sharing—that's important to me because we certainly need a lot of that in this world. My idea for spirituality is to grow that as much as I can so that I am more able to serve others.

MELISSA: There are a couple of things I want to get to before we run out of time, and one is that I know you haven't been writing that long, and I'm actually amazed by what you've accomplished in such a short period of time. So, the question is: When are you coming out with a collection?

LOIS: You know, we talked about how our lives are so full, and I've had to re-evaluate that recently. I'm trying to step back in certain areas so I can actually allow myself to take the time and focus. I have a very good friend who is a mentor, and I need to take some of my poems to him so we can collect them into at least a chapbook and begin sending them out. But right now I'm more or less getting them in decent journals and connecting with groups like San Miguel— I try to go to each year's event—they have a fantastic workshop in Mexico that is a sort of stepping stone toward a collection. As well, Pascale Petit, has put together a fantastic online poetry course called *Toward A Collection*, which has all of the elements from start to finish. I have such a standard. It's very difficult.

You know, my appreciation grows, and it continues to grow, so it's challenging to keep up with what I would feel really good about putting together now. I'm not in a hurry. A poet I interviewed recently took fourteen years to put together a collection, and it's a knockout. I might just be a one book woman.

Photograph by Scott Lutz

Melissa Studdard is the author of the bestselling novel, *Six Weeks to Yehidah*, which was a recipient of the Forward National Literature Award, among other accolades. She is also a mother, a professor, a poet, a reviewer, an editor, and a talk show host. You can learn more about Melissa and her work at www.melissastuddard.com.

Photograph by Denise Winters

Donna Baier Stein is publisher of *Tiferet: Literature, Art, & The Creative Spirit*. Her writing has appeared in *Virginia Quarterly Review, Prairie Schooner* and many other journals and anthologies. Her story collection was a finalist in the Iowa Fiction Awards and her novel received the PEN/New England Discovery Award. She has an MFA from Johns Hopkins University Writing Seminars. She was a founding editor of *Bellevue Literary Review* and is also a freelance copywriter.